WHAT DOES IT TAKE TO LIVE
A LIFE OF
SIGNIFICANCE?

FINDING
YOUR PATH TO
SIGNIFICANCE

UN
COMI

TONY DUNGY

WITH NATHAN WHITAKER

TYNDALE HOUSE PUBLISHERS, INC.
CAROL STREAM, ILLINOIS

ION

Visit Tyndale's exciting Web site at www.tyndale.com

TYNDALE and Tyndale's quill logo are registered trademarks of Tyndale House Publishers, Inc.

Uncommon: Finding Your Path to Significance

Designed by Dean H. Renninger

Published in association with the literary agency of Legacy, LLC, Winter Park, Florida 32789.

Library of Congress Cataloging-in-Publication Data

Dungy, Tony.
   Uncommon : finding your path to significance / Tony Dungy with Nathan Whitaker.
     p. cm.
   ISBN 978-1-4143-2681-8 (hc)
   1. Conduct of life.   2. Dungy, Tony.   3. Football coaches—United States—Anecdotes.
I. Whitaker, Nathan. II. Title.
   BJ1581.2.D864 2009
   170'.44—dc22   2008046798

Printed in the United States of America

15   14   13   12   11   10   09

7   6   5   4

*To my sons, that they might continue
on their journey to becoming uncommon men.*
TONY DUNGY

*To my daughters, that they might hold out for
someday spending their lives with uncommon men.*
NATHAN WHITAKER

CONTENTS

ACKNOWLEDGMENTS IX

INTRODUCTION XI

PART I: DEVELOP YOUR CORE 1

1: Character 3

2: Honesty and Integrity 9

3: Humility and Stewardship 17

4: Courage 29

PART II: LOVE YOUR FAMILY 37

5: How to Treat a Woman 39

6: Fatherhood 51

7: Respect Authority 65

PART III: LIFT YOUR FRIENDS AND OTHERS 75

8: Friendship 77

9: Taking Counsel 83

10: The Power of Positive Influence 89

11: Mentoring 95

PART IV: YOUR FULL POTENTIAL 101

12: Powerful Thoughts 103

13: Education and Athletics 111

14: Career, Work, and Money 117

15: Goals and Risk 125

16: Alcohol and Drugs 131

17: Failure 137

PART V: **ESTABLISH A MISSION THAT MATTERS** 143

18: Style versus Substance 145

19: Priorities 151

20: Being versus Doing 157

21: Following Your Dreams 161

22: Creating Balance 167

PART VI: **CHOOSE INFLUENCE OVER IMAGE** 173

23: Respect for Yourself and Others 175

24: Sexual Integrity 179

25: Platforms 187

26: Role Model 191

PART VII: **LIVE YOUR FAITH** 197

27: Eternal Self-Esteem 199

28: Relationship with Christ 203

29: Faith 207

30: Purpose 211

31: Significance 215

EPILOGUE 221

Q&A WITH COACH DUNGY 225

ABOUT THE AUTHORS 259

ACKNOWLEDGMENTS

THE AUTHORS GRATEFULLY ACKNOWLEDGE the contributions of many who have gone before, those who built into our lives and made this book and its contents possible. In particular, we are grateful for the time and input of Jim Caldwell, Mark Merrill, John Ondrasik, Ken Whitten, and Alan Williams.

Once again, the good people of Tyndale House Publishers, including Lisa Jackson, Jan Long Harris, and Doug Knox, were tremendously helpful in seeing this project through, as was our literary agent, D. J. Snell.

We are especially thankful for Lauren, Amy, and our families, who allowed us the time to undertake yet another book on a tight schedule. And finally, we are grateful to our fathers: to Scott Whitaker, for modeling these *uncommon* qualities to Nathan and assisting with his part of the manuscript; and to Wilbur Dungy, whose *uncommon* life provided the impetus for this project and whose spirit guided it throughout.

INTRODUCTION

Not all those who wander are lost.
  J. R. R. TOLKIEN

SINCE COMING TO INDIANAPOLIS, I have become friends with two young men. Although they grew up fairly close to each other, they were raised under very different circumstances, in totally different environments. Brandon Robinson is white. He grew up in a two-parent home in rural Indiana. Dallas Clifton is black and was raised by his mother in the heart of Indianapolis.

Despite these different backgrounds, however, both boys have a lot in common. Both are extremely bright and articulate and have fun, engaging personalities. Both are good hearted and good looking—the type of young men you hope your daughter will bring home one day. But Brandon and Dallas also have one more thing in common. Both are in prison—the result of making poor decisions they will regret the rest of their lives.

Sadly, stories like Brandon's and Dallas's are becoming more and more common today. In Marion County, Indiana, which includes the city of Indianapolis, there were 8,949 juvenile arrests in 2007. In other words, an average of twenty-five teenagers were arrested on any given day for crimes ranging from disorderly conduct to robbery and aggravated assault. When I hear these statistics, my thoughts immediately turn to the scourge of gangs or to street kids without positive direction. But through Brandon and Dallas, I've learned that is not necessarily the case.

Dan and Cheryl Robinson raised Brandon in a very quiet neighborhood in Warsaw, Indiana. According to Brandon, they were very loving and supportive, wanted the best for him, and tried to keep him away from anything that might hinder his development. Despite the fact that he grew up in what would probably be considered ideal conditions, Brandon began rebelling against his parents' authority.

Brandon began experimenting with marijuana and alcohol. It all seemed like harmless fun for him and his buddies, and he enjoyed his status as the guy with the fake ID who could get the alcohol for his underage friends. Harmless fun, that is, until one summer night when he was driving the guys home after drinking.

It was just a short ride on a road Brandon knew very well. But that night he failed to stop at a stop sign; entered the intersection at sixty miles per hour in his dual-wheeled, extended-cab pickup truck; hit a car; and killed three people, seriously injuring two others. His actions—and their tragic effects—were caused by a blood alcohol level of at least 0.099 percent, well above Indiana's legal limit of 0.08 percent. He was convicted of three counts of driving while intoxicated causing death and two counts of driving while intoxicated causing serious bodily injury. The judge sentenced him to twenty-eight years in prison.

The lives of three people ended that night, and the lives of the two surviving passengers, as well as all the families, forever changed at that moment.

Dallas's story is different, yet the same. From the very start, Alicia Clifton knew Dallas was special. Dallas's sister played the piano, and he often imitated her. By the time he was four, he was playing with both hands, and when he started taking lessons, he progressed faster than anyone could believe. By fifteen, he was playing classical music, writing his own songs, and winning numerous talent contests in and around Indianapolis.

Alicia encouraged Dallas to develop his talent, but she also wanted him to stay grounded in his Christian faith. When he began playing keyboards for several local church choirs, it seemed the ideal way for him to do both.

After a while, however, Alicia began to worry about Dallas. She knew he was paid well for his playing, but he seemed to have too much money at times. Where was he getting it? The answer, she later found out, was through gambling.

The gambling started in elementary school when the older kids taught him how to play a game called "tonk." Soon the penny-ante card games gave way to dice. Craps was easy for Dallas, and he could turn $50 he received from playing at a wedding into $150 or $200 in what seemed like minutes. On top of that, gambling was fun, a real adrenaline rush when things were going well. Of course, Dallas didn't always win, but he always made up those occasional losses the next time. And the winning made a lot of good things happen—he could help his mother pay the bills and buy some nice things for his sisters. He had money to spend on new clothes and gifts for girls, which made him even more popular at school.

When Alicia eventually found out where this extra money was coming from, she warned Dallas about the decisions he was making and the chances he was taking with his life. But everything was going so well for Dallas, he was sure his mom was worrying for no reason.

Dallas graduated from high school and enrolled in a university in Kentucky, attending on a music scholarship. Early in his freshman year, he returned to Indianapolis during a break in classes and decided to find a dice game to pass the time. He figured he could use a little extra spending money at school, and he missed the thrill of the game. Unfortunately, this day happened to be one of those "losing" days. When he lost about $200, he borrowed it from one of the other players, feeling sure his luck would change and he would win it back. But this day, his luck didn't change. Now not only had he lost *his* money, but he had compounded his problems by losing the money he had borrowed. Dallas had to head back to school, but the "friend" who loaned him the money expected to be repaid quickly. He told Dallas that if he didn't get the money from him, he would get it from his family, one way or another.

Worried about what might happen to his mom or his sisters once he was back at school, Dallas had a dilemma. Where could he get some quick cash and put this problem behind him? He could have tried to borrow from someone else, or he could have asked for help from his mother or someone at church. But he didn't. He figured he had gotten himself into this, and he needed to get himself out.

Dallas knew that most people in the underground world of these dice and other gambling games didn't use banks for their holdings, but kept large sums with them. As a result, he got a gun and held up someone who was leaving another dice game. He just needed the money so he could get back to school and stop worrying, but rather than stop the slide, he continued the downward spiral. He knew it wasn't the right thing to do, but he figured it was the only way he could protect his family.

That decision made Dallas one of those Marion County statistics—a teenager arrested. Dallas didn't think his victim would go to the police, but he did. At the age of nineteen, this college student, classical pianist, and church keyboardist was sentenced to five years in prison for armed robbery.

Brandon and Dallas were really my motivation to write this book. Two boys, two different backgrounds, two different upbringings. Both followed the "wide road" and ended up in prison, which tells me that our society today is facing a widespread problem. It's not an inner-city problem, or an economic problem, or even a religious problem. The kind of ideas that our young people are buying into and the pressure to conform are causing our teenagers to follow that path of least resistance.

It's easy to get swept along, borne by the current with no idea where you're headed. Sometimes you find yourself miles out from shore with the lighthouse no longer visible. I've seen it over and over through the years, and I've even felt the pull myself. There have been plenty of times when I've looked around and wondered, *Now how did I get here? Where is* here? *And who are these people floating alongside me?*

Unfortunately, that seems to be the path that way too many of us naturally take. We live in a world in which things are accepted as normal without any thought as to whether they should be or whether there might be a better way. Too often we resign ourselves to accepting that things just are the way they are.

We get pulled in every direction by people and society. Everyone has a different expectation for us as men: be a provider, be tough, be sensitive, don't cry, stay home, go to work, change diapers, go hang out with the boys, *don't* go hang out with the boys, and so on.

Young men today are told to demand respect, be a "gangsta," take no prisoners whether on the streets or in bed, look out for number one. Some have said that being a man today means to be sensitive and caring, to be nurturing, quick to comfort, open to talk. Still others have said that we've been created to explore caves and beat our chests in some sort of masculine cosmic rhythm.

But what does it really mean to *be a man*?

I say this: being a man is more than leaving our wives husbandless, our children fatherless, our employers passionless, our families hopeless.

You can be more. You were created to be more—and better. The messages of the world are a cop-out: the messages of sexual conquest, of financial achievement, of victory in general. Not only are these messages not fair, but they also fall so far short of what you can do—and more importantly, who you can be.

✣　✣　✣

In football, we often speak in terms of keys. We'll key on the quarterback or on a particularly dangerous and game-changing running back. The strong safety keys off of the tight end. On offense, the center may use the middle linebacker as his key for determining whom to block, or the receiver may key off whether the cornerback is playing up on him or back, inside or outside, to determine which way he's going to release from the line of scrimmage to run his route.

Sometimes we refer to it as "finding our landmarks." I've always loved that phrase, for all that it says about football and life. Defensive backs in particular have to find their landmarks in order to properly defend their territory. They are charged with being in a certain place that is dictated by both the offense and the field itself. Their "spot" is determined by how far they are from the end zone, how far from the sideline, and what kind of help they can expect from teammates.

I think our journey as men is similar. We live in a world that is fluid: some of us are single, some are married, some have children at home, some have children away at school, and others see their children only on court-prescribed visitation days. Some of us are nearing the end of our time on earth (we assume), while others of us have our entire lives ahead of us (again, we assume!).

The fundamentals, however, don't change: the keys to life, those landmarks that we can use to find our footing and maintain our position and bearings, will always remain. In football, when our team isn't playing well, I might say, "We have to get back to our fundamentals," referring to those basic principles that allow us to play the game successfully—

blocking, tackling, running, catching. Right now, our society also needs to get back to the fundamentals, those basic principles that will allow us to succeed as men. We can be certain there will always be obstacles along the way. However, having those fundamentals to fall back on will help us to overcome those obstacles. We are not only *able* to effect this change, but I think we *need* to.

This book came about in response to two separate but related causes: First, after writing *Quiet Strength* in 2007, I received a number of letters and e-mails from men—young men, in particular—who said that they are struggling with what it means to truly be a man in this day and age. Second, I've watched young men come into the NFL for the last three decades, but lately it seems they're coming to us less prepared and in need of more direction.

I told our team when we assembled in late 2005, "Continue being who you are, because our young people need to hear from you. If anything, be bolder in who you are, because our boys are getting a lot of wrong messages today about what it means to be a man in this world, about how they should act and talk and dress and treat people. They aren't always getting the right message, but you guys have the right message, and you live it, and we need you to continue to do that." I still believe that.

Though I don't pretend to have all the answers, I hope this book will help you think about where you're headed. Often the path isn't clear and the keys aren't obvious. I realize that many of these topics are deep, complex issues. And you'll probably notice that most of my thoughts come from what I believe the Bible says it takes to be a man. I won't apologize for or shy away from that, because that's the way I was raised, and God's Word has always been the best source of advice for me.

At the end of the day, I'm sure of one thing: accumulating stuff and women and titles and money are wrong keys. Fitting in, following the crowd, and being common are not what we're supposed to do. There's more in store for us.

My football coach at the University of Minnesota, Cal Stoll, often told us, "Success is uncommon, therefore not to be enjoyed by the common man. I'm looking for uncommon people."

That should be true for the rest of us as well. Over the next few pages, I hope we can figure out what it means to be a man.

A true man, one who is *uncommon*.

PART I

DEVELOP YOUR CORE

+ + +

Experience is the
name everyone gives
to their mistakes.

OSCAR WILDE

CHAPTER 1

CHARACTER

Educating the mind without educating the heart is no education at all.
    ARISTOTLE

IN 1998, THE INDIANAPOLIS COLTS were confronted
with a dilemma. Finishing the prior season with three wins
against thirteen defeats, they held the first pick in the NFL
draft that April. Their selection would affect the direction of
the team for years to come, positively or negatively. At the
time, I was head coach of the Tampa Bay Buccaneers, so I was
worried about my team in Tampa, and didn't realize what a
huge impact the Colts' selection would have on my life.

Bill Polian, president of the Colts, was faced with a dif-
ficult choice between two great talents: Ryan Leaf and Peyton
Manning. Both were big players with strong arms: Leaf had
set numerous records at Washington State University, and
Manning had done the same at the University of Tennessee.
In hindsight, it seems like an obvious choice, but at the

time there was plenty of debate. Media analysts and scouts around the league were split evenly, but Bill decided to select Manning. There was no question Peyton had the physical skills to be a great player, but what tipped the scales in Bill's mind were Peyton's work ethic, his love for the game, his approach toward football as a job, and his quiet private life. Ultimately, when faced with the choice that would define the course of the franchise, the Colts based that decision on character, and that choice has resulted in great success for us and for our future Hall of Fame quarterback.

For the Colts, character is a quality that can be measured just like height, weight, and speed. In fact, we put more emphasis on this area than we do on physical tools. Coaching ability or talent cannot make up for a lack of character. In the draft, there are only a few things that will knock a player out of consideration for our team, and this issue of character is one of them. We have a category on our evaluation form that is labeled "DNDC"—*Do Not Draft because of Character.* Every year, many players that we put in that category get drafted in the first round by other teams, and some even go on to become household names in the NFL. But we pass on them because of something we see in their character that makes us believe they are not worth the risk. Most of the time, we're right. And those times when we are make it worth even those times when we're not.

That's not necessarily the common approach today, though. So often there is such an emphasis on results that it doesn't matter how you get them. Moving up is more important than *the way* you move up. It doesn't matter what kind of person you are, just what kind of player you are. It doesn't matter if you follow the rules or break them, just as long as you come out on top. After all, that's what everyone will remember at the end of the day. That's why we have to have steroid testing in the NFL. That's why medals are forfeited in the Olympics. Competitors have to ask themselves: *Since everyone is doing it, if I want to have a legitimate chance, I have to do it too, right?*

What you do is not as important as how you do it. Those are the words that keep coming back to me when I am tempted to choose what is expedient over what is right. People who bend the rules to get ahead usually get caught in the long run. But even if they don't get caught, they will always know how they made it to the top. And at some deep-down level, they'll know that they're frauds and that maybe they didn't have what it took to accomplish such achievements on a level playing field.

The other problem is that, at some point, somebody who *does* care how the game is played—a boss, a board of directors—may well find out. For me as an employer, *how* you do your job has always been more important than *what* you do. Can you be counted on to do things the right way? Do you have the appropriate habits to get you through a tough situation, or are you the type to cut corners and hope things turn out all right? Your character will determine the answer.

When I was growing up, my folks were very clear about the importance of character. "Your word is your bond," my mom would say constantly. The thought that someone might think of her as unreliable or untrustworthy was the worst thing possible. That's how she taught us to choose our friends—not by where they lived or what their parents did for a living. She wanted us to have friends we could trust.

Today, I have friends of all ages, races, and economic

backgrounds. But my closest friends are people of high character—and I don't hang around with people I can't trust.

My mom believed that a person's character reveals what
he or she really believes about life. It it important to be honest? Is it important to obey your parents all the time, or just
important not to get caught disobeying? Is there a God who
really rewards good character, or is it okay to do whatever it
takes to win?

That motherly guidance has impacted me professionally
as well. Because of the premium my mom put on character,
I look for it in the people I work with. My style in creating a
coaching staff is to hire talented coaches and teachers and let
them do their jobs. This means that I have to have people I
can trust implicitly, because I'm not going to spend my time
checking on them. I don't want coaches or players who are not
going to represent us well, either on or off the field.

Character begins with the little things in life. I must show
that I can be trusted with each and every thing, no matter
how trivial it may seem. By the time I was a teenager, my dad
let me stay out pretty late playing basketball with my friends.
It didn't happen right away—I couldn't be out at midnight
when I was thirteen. But gradually, my parents gave me a
little more freedom—and usually with someone they knew
would keep an eye on me. By the time I was sixteen or seventeen, they knew that if I said I was playing ball with my
buddies in East Lansing or Ann Arbor, that's exactly what I
was doing and I wasn't involved in anything that could get
me in trouble. They had watched me grow and had given me
enough opportunities to test my character that, by then, they
knew they could trust me.

"Character may be manifested in the great moments, but

it is made in the small ones," wrote Phillips Brooks, an American clergyman in the 1800s. Over time, we create ourselves and build our character through the little acts we do.

When it comes to character, the game of football can be a real *test* for our players. During any given season, they will have many moments when their character will be challenged. Will they decide to do the right thing, even when they know doing so will be difficult?

Character can also be *revealed* at those same crossroads: what are the values that guide the decisions these players make in their day-to-day lives? Training camp reveals them early. A person's reaction to winning, success, fame, recognition, and acceptance reveals character. Would you rather be described as successful and famous or as honest, forgiving, faithful, trustworthy, understanding of others, reasonable, thoughtful, and personally accountable?

Character is tested, revealed, and further *developed* by the decisions we make in the most challenging times. We have to know what is right, and we have to choose to do it. That is how character is developed—by facing those decisions and choosing the right way over and over until it becomes second nature. It's just how you do things.

Outwardly, character reflects an inner life committed to honor and uncompromising integrity. If we haven't allowed our players, subordinates, or children to grow into those values and learn to be accountable for themselves, then we have done them a disservice.

Albert Camus once said, "Integrity has no need of rules." I tend to agree. I don't have very many team rules for our players. They know where I stand on things, and they know that there are consequences for breaking the rules that we do have. I try to apply one set of rules uniformly for our team, while keeping in mind that the players are individuals and come from different life experiences. Really, it's not any different from what I do with my children.

Ultimately, character and its growth don't come from rules but from the small actions of responsibility that occur day after day. That's why I believe it's important to give our players a certain amount of freedom—and the responsibility that goes with it—to allow growth to take place. In the end, character is a blend of inner courage, wisdom, and a sense of duty to yourself, to others, and to something greater than you.

In a common world, becoming an uncommon man begins by cultivating uncommon character.

CHAPTER 2

HONESTY AND INTEGRITY

Honesty is the first chapter in the book of wisdom.
THOMAS JEFFERSON

WHEN I WAS GROWING UP, the rules in our home were set in stone. If there was a rule, we knew we had better follow it. An interesting corollary to that, however, was that honesty had a way of mitigating any punishment to come. As a boy, I thought that my dad had coined the phrase "the truth shall set you free," but when I got older, I learned he was actually quoting Jesus.

Home is where I first learned the concept of "no excuses, no explanations." If I came home after my curfew, I knew I was better off telling my parents the truth. They were still upset, but the punishment was always less than when I made up an excuse. And my dad must have had spies out there in the streets, because he always knew exactly what I had been doing anyway. Everything took a backseat to honesty in my parents' book.

Skirting the rules will come back to hurt you. Whether it's doing something illegal or cheating on a test rather than actually learning the material, you may get the edge and experience a short-term "win," but dishonesty will eventually catch up with you.

This idea was tested on my first day as a student at the University of Minnesota. My very first class was Psychology 1001, which met Mondays, Wednesdays, and Fridays for a large lecture, and then in small groups on Tuesdays and Thursdays with a teaching assistant to discuss the points made in the lecture. As I walked into class the first Monday, I was confronted by a guy with a box of materials. In the box he had the class notes—for the whole quarter—and he was selling them for twenty dollars. A long line of people were waiting to buy them, but I was a little naive—and cheap.

"Are you on the teaching staff?" I asked. He said he wasn't. "Is it required that students buy these?"

"No, I'm selling the notes so you won't have to go to the lectures. Just go to the two weekly small-group discussions."

I pressed on, not hiding my skepticism. "How do you get the notes before class?" I asked. "What if he goes over some other things?"

"The professor is on video; the material never changes." As we were talking, he continued to sell. It appeared that most of the students were getting the notes, but I was still unsure, so I proceeded into the classroom. Sure enough, the professor was on a big screen. After class, the guy was once again waiting outside, now surrounded by a crush of students. His market had increased once students saw the video. Multiple thoughts raced through my mind: *What if these aren't complete notes? What if some things were left out? If they are good notes, is this cheating because I didn't really take them?* And the kicker was, I knew that if my dad were teaching this class, he would have come in live one day just to keep everyone on their toes.

But everybody was getting the notes. I thought maybe this was the way it was done in college. I worried that I'd be at a *disadvantage* if I didn't have them—I couldn't let that happen. In one hour I went from not even considering buying the notes to rationalizing why I *had* to have them. I bought the notes that day, but as I was going to my next class, I began to have second thoughts. This wasn't right. I tried to convince myself they were just an aid to help me do better in class. They were available to everyone, so using them wasn't really cheating. But deep inside, I knew that, as teachers, my mom and dad wouldn't approve of this. Go to class, take your own notes, get your own A. So I rationalized again: *I'll just use the notes as a backup. I'll still go to the lectures and get the material myself.*

I can tell you that as the quarter progressed and the weather got colder in Minneapolis, I was tempted several times not to go to class, especially when I saw that the notes were pretty thorough. I didn't skip, though, as I was always afraid that the professor might show up one day. And more than that, there was just something inside me—something my parents had instilled—that made me feel it wouldn't be quite right not to go. My mother's words kept coming back to me: *It's sometimes easier to do the wrong thing, but it's always better to do the right thing.*

That's life. That's integrity. The choice between what's convenient and what's right. The lingering effect is that this choice carries longer-term consequences than we realize at the time. I believe it was Abraham Lincoln who said that you can fool all of the people some of the time, and some of the people all of the time, but you cannot fool all of the people all of the time. It's a burden and reputation you do not want.

Integrity is what you do when no one is watching; it's doing the right thing all the time, even when it may work to your disadvantage. Integrity is keeping your word. Integrity is that internal compass and rudder that directs you to where you know you should go when everything around you is pulling you in a different direction. Some people think reputation is the same thing as integrity, but they are different. Your reputation is the public perception of your integrity. Because it's other people's opinions of you, it may or may not be accurate. Others determine your reputation, but only *you* determine your integrity.

Integrity is critical to everything we do because it is the foundation of trustworthiness in our own eyes, in the eyes of those around us, and in God's eyes. Can I count on you to be my teammate, perform your assignment, and do your work in the weight room in the off-season? Will you put in the necessary time to analyze film and learn the game plan? Can I count on you to be my business partner, or do I have to keep one eye on you while I'm trying to serve the customers? Can I count on you to be my marriage partner? Do you mean what you say when we exchange those wedding vows, or is it only for better . . . and for better? Do I have to worry about you having an affair because you aren't honest in other areas of your life? Can I count on you to do what you say you will do, no matter what may come along to make it difficult?

Much of my work is dependent upon things that my players and coaches do when no one is watching them. I suppose I could watch as much as possible, but I don't like micromanaging. It's just not an efficient use of my time. And at the end of the day, if I'm going to help those around me grow as people, they are going to have to take responsibility for what they do when I'm not watching.

Integrity is also a critical element in any marriage. For me, it means doing everything I can to make sure that Lauren is comfortable and confident. The nature of my job, the hours that I put in at work, and the number of times I'm away from home create enough hardships for her; I don't want to add to that by causing her worry or stress.

When I'm at training camp for three and a half weeks every year, Lauren has to do everything by herself at home. Our camp schedule includes a lot of late meetings, so we don't even get to talk as much as we usually do. Just being apart is taxing enough, but if she had to wonder what I was doing at night—if I was secretly seeing another woman, if I was out partying with the guys—it would add that much more stress. So I do everything I can to make sure that Lauren has complete confidence in me and our relationship.

Every year at the end of June, I head up to northern Minnesota on a spiritual retreat with a group of coaches. We're there over the weekend, and we stay in an area that gets lousy mobile phone reception. Lauren knows a lot of the coaches involved, and because of the history of honesty I've built with her, she never worries about what I'm doing or whom I am with.

That level of trust has helped us in a lot of ways—even in making the decision to move the family back to Florida while I work in Indianapolis. We were able to simply analyze the decision in light of the pluses and minuses for our kids and not have to factor in any apprehensions about our relationship.

The great thing about integrity is that it is truly no respecter of position or wealth or race or gender. It is not determined by shifting circumstances, cultural dynamics, or what you've previously achieved. From the moment you are born, you—and you alone—determine whether you will be a person of integrity. Integrity does not come in degrees—low, medium, or high. You either have integrity or you do not.

In the Old Testament, Daniel was an adviser to King Darius. The other nobles in the kingdom were envious of his stature with the king and were committed to finding something wrong in him to bring about his downfall, "but they couldn't find anything to criticize or condemn. He was faithful, always responsible, and completely trustworthy."[1]

We should live our lives like Daniel, so that if we ever had an FBI background check or a newspaper reporter digging into our personal lives, they would not only find no "dirt" on us but also find us to be honest and trustworthy. This was driven home to me when I was appointed to the President's Council on Service and Civic Participation. We had an FBI background check done on us, which included filling out a waiver to allow the search, and then being asked numerous questions like, "Have you ever been arrested?" "Have you ever been convicted of a felony?" "Has your tax return ever been audited?" and so on. The final question really caused me to think: "Have you ever done anything that would be embarrassing for the president of the United States to be associated with?" I understood why they asked that question, but when I realized that I had done many things I wouldn't want even *my parents* to be associated with, I wished I had worked a little harder in the area of integrity.

When it is all said and done, my reputation doesn't mat-

---

[1] Daniel 6:4

ter. It's important, but what others think of me is simply out of my control. What does matter, however, is what I think of me. My integrity. That is something I can control—by taking care of the little things, day in and day out, when no one is watching.

Because I am—and God is.

CHAPTER 3

HUMILITY AND STEWARDSHIP

We can't all be heroes because somebody has to sit on the curb and clap as they go by.
    WILL ROGERS

MORE AND MORE, as new players come into the league each year, I see what appears to be—for lack of a better descriptor—a "look at me" attitude. It doesn't seem to be driven by ego as much as by a struggle to survive in a world with a finite number of positions, where so many stand ready to take your place. I think it's further driven into our guys that the more "*SportsCenter* moments" they have, the more they will be worth to their team—and the more money they'll get paid. Guys will justify their attitudes by saying that if they don't blow their own horns, nobody will. Management books seem to say that this applies to other professions as well.

The problem is that nobody really listens when we blow our own horns; after all, we're biased. Also, it's pretty unbecoming. I think that's why my mother always told me never to do it. She may have been thinking of the admonition in Proverbs 27:2, which says, "Let someone else praise you, not your own mouth—a stranger, not your own lips."

Muhammad Ali, however, had the opposite effect on a lot of guys in my generation. "I am the greatest" was his signature line, and the more he said it, the more people came to watch him. Many of them came hoping to see him get beaten, which didn't bother him—the more people came, the more he got paid. He had supreme confidence in his ability, and he was just trying to raise some hype in order to increase ticket sales. It was an era in which not many black men had been able to stand up and be bold in that kind of way, and Ali soon became an icon in the African American community.

In the same way, Joe Namath guaranteed a victory in Super Bowl III, pulled it off, and became a larger-than-life figure in NFL football. Both Ali and Namath came along just as sports television was really growing, and they were just what this new venue needed—attractions. As my generation watched, the idea of the humble athlete, the guy who let his play on the field do his talking, began to be chipped away. The media seemed to like the guys who provided the highlight, the sound bite.

As a society, we claim that we like the quiet, humble athlete, but in reality, those aren't the guys who get the focus—at least not as much as the guys who are trying to bring attention to their own names. Barry Sanders and Deion Sanders came into the NFL together in 1989. Barry was "old school." He did his job and played spectacular football, and when he scored a touchdown, he handed the ball to the official and then went back to the bench.

After games, it was hard to get him to talk about himself.

He would praise his offensive linemen, then head out and stay away from the cameras as much as possible. As great as Barry Sanders was and as much as we admired his skill on the field, the media tended to gravitate more toward Deion Sanders, the self-proclaimed "Prime Time." Deion was flashy, loud, and proud. He played great and was always ready to put on a show, especially for the cameras. Behind the scenes, Barry and Deion probably weren't much different. Everyone who played with Deion said he was hardworking, a great teammate, and not really like the "Prime Time" persona he was known for. But Deion had figured out that in our society, flash sells. He had endorsements, shoe and clothing lines, and notoriety.

But there's a problem with this. There is a proverb that says, "Pride goes before destruction."[2] Time and time again we see examples where the fine line between confidence and pride has been blurred, resulting in fall after fall. Pride is all about me, but confidence is a realization that God has given me abilities and created me to fill a unique role that no one else is called to fill. Borne in humility, confidence is a recognition that life is not about me but about using the gifts and abilities I have been blessed with to their fullest. And it's not just using the gifts to benefit me, but to help my team and impact others.

I appreciate that form of humility; it's not a false modesty claiming that what you accomplished or who you are isn't important, but a realization that God created all of us with unique gifts and abilities. It's a different dynamic than tearing myself down; rather, it's trying to lift others up. It's embracing the idea that God created me for a particular place and time, and sharing that idea with others who were also created to

---

[2] Proverbs 16:18

play a role. Once you can do that, it becomes much easier to let go of status or false ideas of respect.

My first season in Tampa, my brother-in-law Loren came down for one of our early home games. He tells the story better than I do:[3]

It was September 1996, and Tony had invited me down to see my first game in Tampa against Seattle. I was excited and got in early so I could experience everything that weekend. Tony and I drove to the hotel on Saturday afternoon and put our bags in the suite that the team had reserved for him. As I understand it, many coaches hold meetings with their staff on Saturday night in the living room—that's why they have a suite.

We got settled and checked some college-game scores, then headed downstairs for chapel and meetings with the team. Afterward, Tony went back up to the room, but I stayed downstairs. I had already eaten dinner with the team before chapel, but I heard they had a snack before bed, and I thought that seemed like a good idea too.

It turns out that a "snack" is yet another full meal in the NFL—after eating and watching some of the college games with the players, I headed back up to the room. The entire suite was dark. I should have known that Tony wasn't going to tweak or second-guess the plan they had put together all week. I felt around in the dark for the pullout bed in the living room, climbed in . . . and found Tony already there, asleep.

---

[3] Both Loren and Nathan wanted to include this story in *Quiet Strength*, but I refused. After all, it's awkward to note in the first person your own humility. Plus, telling it just didn't seem very . . . quiet. This time they insisted, so as a compromise, we've included the story in Loren's words.

*He woke up and we began a vigorous discussion about
who was going to get the bedroom.*

*"You're my guest; you take it," he said. "Seriously,
Loren, I invited you to Tampa."*

*"You're kidding, right? You're the head coach of the
Buccaneers with a game tomorrow, and I'm the relative
eating free food and staying in a free room—you take it!"*

*This went on longer than it should have. Tony refused
to leave, and of course, so did I. After all, not only was it
the right thing, but I knew I would have to answer to my
sister if Tony slept on a pullout bed the night before a game.
Finally, I just lay down on the floor in the living room and
threatened to sleep there for the night unless he left and took
the bedroom.*

Rather than insisting that others respect us, we need to
make sure that *we* are respecting others, holding *others* in the
proper esteem. We need to make sure that we demonstrate a
respect for others simply because they are here, trying their
best to be all they were created to be. Those who truly live
out that quality will make the best spouses, teammates, parents, friends, and business partners. Stop for a moment and
think about people you know who tried and are trying to be
all they should be. Are we modeling that for our children?
Hopefully we're teaching them that humility—that life is not
about us but about others and something greater than us—is
to be valued.

Important but Not Indispensable

My dad, Wilbur Dungy, had a Ph.D. in physiology that he had
earned from Michigan State University. When introducing

himself, however, he was always "Wil Dungy." I never thought anything about it, really; that was just who he was.

I know a federal judge who has been on the bench for more than thirty years. He was appointed by President Richard Nixon and has decided cases on subjects covering everything from death-row issues to busing in Florida's public schools. Yet every time he meets someone, he introduces himself simply as "Terry." Those who have seen him in action on a daily basis call him "Your Honor," because it feels right to refer to him with that title of respect, but he would never insist on it. He has an inherent and contagious humility in regard to the role he has been appointed to and the life he has been called to live. His sense that "we're all in this together, but we simply have different roles" is what makes him so well respected in the legal community and society at large, as well as by his family and all who personally know him. If he insisted on a title, that would chip away at how he is viewed by others.

Over time, blowing your own horn ends up backfiring and chipping away at any respect you might think you deserve.

Chuck Noll, football Hall of Fame coach of the Pittsburgh Steelers from 1969 to 1991 and winner of four Super Bowls, gave me my start in the NFL, both as a player and later as a coach. Coach Noll had a great way of keeping everything in perspective on those legendary Steeler teams of the 1970s. He used to assure us both with words and by the way he treated us that every player was important ("We need every man on the roster to win"), but he also made it abundantly clear that no one was indispensable. We knew that if one of our star players was injured, we could still play well and still win. So even though we had many Hall of Fame players, our games were never about individual accomplishments. Teamwork was valued above all. It was not about "I" or "me" but about "us" and "we."

This was the primary reason that Coach Noll brought in assistant coaches from the college ranks. Similarly, when he traded players away (like me!), he always looked to get draft picks in return, not players from other teams. He wanted people who would buy into the "Steeler Way" and not try to bring other ideas into play. Other teams may have good ideas that work well for them, but we would win the Steeler Way. And every Steeler believed that, which is one of the reasons we were so successful.

None of us was ever left thinking that he was the most important piece of the puzzle, but rather that he was a significant piece and that every piece was an important and necessary element to achieve the team's goals. I've found over the years that such a perspective is a much healthier and less pressurized way to view myself: important but not indispensable.

Sports have always given us great pictures of true humility: I think of Art Rooney Sr., the founder of the Steelers. When I came to the team in 1977, he still lived in the same inner-city Pittsburgh house he had always lived in. He walked to work and spent time with everyone in the neighborhood even though he owned the football team. To the neighbors, he was simply their friend, Art Rooney. When the Steelers went to their first Super Bowl in New Orleans, he was adamant that he didn't want the limousine that was customarily provided for the owner of the team during the week. He would do what he had always done—ride the team bus or call a cab if he needed to. That was Mr. Rooney, and he was not going to change just because his team was now in the Super

Bowl spotlight. On the other side of the coin, I know a public relations director of a professional sports team who lost his job in part because he failed to use *all* the various titles of one of the team executives in a publicity release. I can't imagine that kind of thing bothering Mr. Rooney; his example left an impression on anybody who ever worked for the Steelers, including me. That's one of the reasons I tried to insist that Loren take that bed at the Marriott.

Submission and Availability

Two men outside of my family come to mind when I think of the submission and availability of a humble heart: Coach Tom Landry and Reverend Billy Graham. Both epitomize humility in every sense of the word.

Coach Landry is no longer with us, but I watched him a lot when I was a young coach. The thing that impressed me the most was that although he was a smart, innovative coach who had a great record, he never seemed to be the center of attention. I learned much from him about this core characteristic of humility. He was a quiet man. At times it seemed he was almost shy, but it was simply his humility before God and man. If you probed, he would eventually tell you that he coached the Dallas Cowboys—but that wouldn't be among the first things he talked about. Instead, he would tell you about his family and then ask about you and yours.

And if you had the chance to hear him speak, you would not list him as one of the most dynamic speakers you have ever heard—just one of the most effective. I have witnessed times when he would begin to speak, quietly and even a bit hesitantly, and I watched as members of the audience slowly leaned forward in their chairs to draw nearer to every word that came from his mouth. Dynamic? No, not at all. Soft-spoken, humble, authentic, appealing? Absolutely. And powerful. This was not his own power, but a power that came from God. Tom Landry's life was not about him; it was one of submission to the God he followed.

The Reverend Billy Graham is similar to Coach Landry in so many ways. Unlike Coach Landry, though, Dr. Graham was a dynamic and vibrant speaker in his prime. He spoke with a clarity and power that introduced millions to his Savior. But despite being one of the most recognizable people in the world, Dr. Graham never felt he was the star. And he would be the first to tell you that it wasn't about him. His power and message came from the God whom he served.

Both began as ordinary men—submitted and available to God—whom God then used to touch the lives of others. Interestingly, that is often how God works: through ordinary, available people who have submitted their lives to Him. He transforms the common work that we do into something majestic and eternal. Something uncommon.

He needs only the simplest of tools—gentle, pure, and humble lives—that are willing to be used in the simple, everyday moments of fathering, coaching, speaking, listening, sharing, and caring.

God used Tom Landry and Billy Graham for great and godly things because they were submitted and available to Him. I suspect He can do the same with each of us.

We all need to remember and reflect upon this idea of humility every day of our lives. I was very fortunate to grow up when I did and come in contact with a lot of men who did great things and were still humble—men like my dad, Art Rooney,

Tom Landry, and Dr. Graham. Unfortunately, I'm concerned that men like this are becoming rarer and rarer.

Stewardship

It seems to be a very natural progression from discussing humility to bringing in the idea of stewardship. Stewardship—like humility—requires a recognition that life is not about us. Specifically, a clear understanding of stewardship not only recognizes that it is not about us but also believes that it is all about God and that it all belongs to and comes from God. This sounds good and is certainly something we can all embrace—at least with our words and intellect—but allowing stewardship to direct the decisions of daily living . . . Well, that is another matter entirely.

For example, if you have investments, how do you feel when the stock market drops? What kind of car have you recently purchased? What do you give to your church? What ministries or charities have you recently decided to invest in? The old saying "show me your checkbook and I'll tell you what's important to you" still rings true today. Where we put our money is one of the telltale indicators as to whether or not we really understand the concept of stewardship.

But stewardship does not just apply to money. It's also about time. What do we do with the twenty-four hours a day we have been given? Stewardship is also about our talents and abilities. What have we done to maximize the gifts and abilities we find within ourselves?

This idea of stewardship is another area where I think our young men have gotten the wrong message over the years. I see it in our players a lot. They are told that because they've worked hard and sacrificed, now that they've made it into professional football, they deserve the rewards that go along with it. And it is tempting to get the nice car and the nice clothes, to acquire some of the things that you've always wanted. There's also a great deal of peer pressure to "look like a professional athlete." But the idea of being a role model, of giving back to the community where you grew up or where you live now, is not talked about much. It doesn't have to be money that you give back. It can be time, encouragement, or simply role modeling—letting our young men know that they don't have to follow the crowd; they don't have to do the stereotypical things. I tell our players that being good role models is one way we can be good stewards of the positions God has put us in. I also try to teach my sons the value of a dollar the way my dad taught me.

Don't get me wrong; I don't have it down as well as I should. I probably never will. Some of the men I've been fortunate to work with in football through the years are far better examples of good stewardship than I am. Their examples haunt me, but they also inspire me. I still have a tendency to make poor choices with my time, procrastinate about improving some area of my life, and hold on to things too tightly as if I owned them, fearing that if I open my hands they will fly away. I should know better, yet I'm continuing to learn that stewardship is not the same as ownership, and it's definitely not about me.

We begin to approach a true understanding of what stewardship is when we realize that everything we have is a gift from God. We are His, and the things we have in our control are His resources *entrusted* to us—for wise usage. Perhaps, I would even add, for wise *eternal* usage. When we begin to see ourselves as the stewards or the trustees of the resources we control—

not the owners—we are on the verge of understanding the true meaning of stewardship, whether those resources are our bodies, abilities, time, or possessions. So if it all comes from Him, I suppose one of the questions He might be asking is this: "Can you be trusted with what I gave you?"

In order to answer that question, you'll need to ask yourself several more: How do I use what I have? Can I be trusted with more? Do I take care of the body He has given me? Do I need a thirty-hour day, or do I simply need to be more efficient and incorporate better priorities in the twenty-four hours I've been given?

And finally, as stewards of all we have within our control, we must ask, Do I invest it in eternity? Do I do things that will outlive me? Do I invest in the lives of others? Do I invest in the expansion of God's agenda?

Stewardship—it's all about Him.

CHAPTER 4

COURAGE

*Twenty years from now you will be more disappointed by the things
you didn't do than by the ones you did do. So throw off the
bowlines. Sail away from the safe harbor. Catch the trade winds
in your sails. Explore. Dream. Discover.*
MARK TWAIN

GETTING UP IN THE MORNING is not for the faint of
heart.

Being a man is not easy, but it never has been, I would
guess. The demands on us are many; the hours in the day are
still capped at twenty-four. We get tugged, second-guessed,
pulled in different directions, and at the end of the day we are
left wondering what happened. And sometimes it seems like
those are the good days.

One of the most important things I have learned along
the way is having the courage to stand by my convictions—
those things that I know are right, those guiding principles

that I know to stick with. Sometimes that means standing out from the crowd or not being popular, but sometimes that's the only responsible place to be. It doesn't necessarily make the days any easier, but at least I feel like I'm still heading in the right direction when the day is over and the next one is on its way.

When I was young, a lot of my high school friends had their lives mapped out: graduate from high school, get a well-paying job in an auto plant, buy a nice car, and maybe get married. The nice car was a definite, though.

However, my parents had always made it clear that my siblings and I were going to college. We simply took it for granted, but there were times when it set us apart. Studying was necessary, both to earn good grades to get into college and to learn the material that we would later need as a foundation for college work. This sometimes put me at odds with my friends, who wanted me to go play ball or just have fun. My parents were okay with those things, but only *after* the studying was done. They set up the rules for me because, at that age, I wouldn't always have had the courage to say, "I can't hang out with you now; I need to study." It was easier to say, "My parents won't let me." But eventually, that ability to stand up on my own would have to grow.

Lynn Swann was one of the finest receivers to ever play the game of football. A star out of Southern Cal, Lynn was a great player for the Steelers.

Lynn also took ballet—not very popular for men in the 1970s. But Lynn felt that ballet would improve his body control and consequently help him become a better football player. In the macho world of pro football, that certainly wasn't the norm, and I know he took a lot of grief for it. But

Lynn didn't care what other people said about his decision to take ballet; he just did it. And that takes real courage—to do what you think is best even when you might be ridiculed for it. Looking back on his four Super Bowl rings and a Hall of Fame career, I'm sure Lynn Swann is glad he didn't give in to the peer pressure back then.

No one is immune to peer pressure, and we're susceptible to it at any age. It's just that as we get older, we do a better job of rationalizing it or hiding it altogether. But through the years, I've learned another way of dealing with it. These days, when it comes to the burden of peer pressure, I make sure I know for myself what is right and am prepared to stick with it. Courage can be demonstrated by standing up to the school bully or intervening to prevent someone you don't know from being hurt. But more often than not, it's the day-to-day moments of reaching down inside yourself to find the courage to stand alone that can be the toughest.

I pay attention to my internal compass. I think it has always been there, guiding me, but as I've matured, I've listened to it better and more often. It helps me stay "lashed to the mast," as Homer wrote of Odysseus doing to keep from being drawn into destruction by the Sirens. That Greek myth resonates because we can relate to that feeling. Even when we know we are heading toward something that could lead to our destruction, it can still seem awfully appealing.

That internal compass, sharpened by having positive peers around me and by studying my Bible, keeps me lashed to the mast.

The Rooney family is one of the pioneers of the National Football League, having owned the Pittsburgh Steelers from the team's inception. The Rooneys have never been afraid to stand by their convictions, whether others were following or not. Bill Nunn was a sportswriter and editor for the *Pittsburgh Courier* (Pittsburgh's African American newspaper) who was known to be critical of the Steelers and specifically their personnel department in the 1960s. After Bill wrote a particularly scathing article in 1967, Dan Rooney responded in a way that was, in typical Dan Rooney fashion, completely uncommon.

He called and invited Bill Nunn to lunch.

During lunch, Dan picked Bill's brain about what he thought would improve the Steelers' approach to personnel. Bill had played basketball at West Virginia State with Chuck Cooper, the first African American to be drafted by a National Basketball Association team, and Earl Lloyd, the first African American to play in an NBA game. He told Dan that the Steelers were overlooking players at the small schools, especially historically black colleges.

So Dan hired him as a scout that year.

In 1969, when Chuck Noll arrived, the Steelers really began to actively mine this talent base. Coach Noll's first Steeler draft pick was Joe Greene of North Texas State, chosen over Terry Hanratty, a quarterback out of Notre Dame, whom Coach Noll was getting a lot of pressure to select (the Steelers ended up getting Hanratty in the second round). In 1970, they added Terry Bradshaw from Louisiana Tech, Ron Shanklin from North Texas State, and Mel Blount from Southern University with their first three picks, and over the years that followed, they took Steve Davis from Delaware State, Dwight White from East Texas State, John Stallworth from Alabama A&M, and Frank Lewis and Bob Barber from Grambling State, all with high selections.

They were not afraid to go find talent at small schools, whether others were looking there or not.

I watched the way the Steelers did things, and it reinforced my instincts to surround myself with those who were best qualified for the job. I had hired Mike Tomlin as an assistant coach in 2001 when I was still the head coach of the Buccaneers. I first met Mike when he was at the University of Cincinnati. He was an energetic, excellent teacher who was extremely bright, and I believed he was destined for a terrific career. Six years later, Mike was finishing his first season as a coordinator in the NFL with the Minnesota Vikings. I was preparing the Colts for Super Bowl XLI when Dan Rooney, who was in the midst of searching for a head coach, called me to talk about Mike.

The Steelers had two excellent candidates already in house—Ken Wisenhunt and Russ Grimm—and most everyone in football expected one of them to get the job. But Dan Rooney has never let other people's expectations determine what is best for his team. I told him all the reasons why I believed Mike would be an excellent head coach. Mike was only thirty-four and had not yet been included on those lists of "hot" potential coaches that seem to be a prerequisite for being hired these days. In fact, many people thought Dan was only interviewing Mike to satisfy the NFL mandate to interview minority candidates. I'm sure he wanted to abide by the rule, but I could tell by my conversation with him that Mike's being black was not the primary reason Dan interviewed him. In spite of the limitations other people saw in Mike, Dan saw a lot of the same qualities he had seen in Chuck Noll and Bill Cowher.

Two weeks later, Dan Rooney announced Mike as the youngest head coach in the NFL and only the third head coach of the Pittsburgh Steelers since 1969. The Rooneys really do stand by their convictions and have done so for decades. And it has taken courage in the face of criticism and contrary views.

The Rooneys were instrumental in my development as well, as they and Coach Noll told me as a first-year coach in 1981 that I needed to be myself. For me, that ended up meaning I could continue to live out my life as a Christian on a daily basis as I began coaching. "God gives you convictions for a reason," they told me.

When I arrived in Kansas City as the defensive backs coach, Marty Schottenheimer had turned the Chiefs around, in part because he was bound and determined to do things his own way. One of those ways involved something very small: staying at the team hotel the night before the game. Or rather, *not* staying at the hotel. Marty didn't believe that it was necessary, and he didn't do it. Even though it was a small thing, I appreciated Marty's willingness to live with the criticism that would come if there was an incident involving his players the night before a game or if his teams didn't play well. He didn't believe it was necessary for coaches to stay in the hotel and therefore wasn't going to require it—even if it would have been safer and helped him to avoid the second-guessing he would suffer if we didn't play well.

We played the Atlanta Falcons recently, and as is our custom, Clyde Christensen, our receivers coach, and I headed out from our team hotel the afternoon before the game for a walk. The hotel was in the downtown area of Atlanta, and before long, we ended up at Ebenezer Baptist Church on Auburn Avenue, the home church of Dr. Martin Luther King Jr. We talked about Dr. King's legacy, his courage, and his uncommon approach to manhood.

Martin Luther King Jr. was a man who stood by his convictions. Regardless of how he was being treated, he stood with dignity, grace, and love.

And courage.

As we walked around Auburn Avenue that morning, I thought about the courage of Dr. King and others who stood shoulder to shoulder with him. Because of them, our black players didn't have to stay in a separate hotel that day. My wife did not have to move to the back of the bus when riding to the game. I could coach in the Super Bowl . . . and sip from the same drinking fountain as Clyde. Because of that courage, Mike Tomlin will never have to worry about finding a restaurant that will serve him in the South, and an old friend of mine, Ernie Cook, was invited to speak to the graduating class of 2008 at Florida State University.

"We will have to repent in this generation not merely for the hateful words and actions of the bad people but for the appalling silence of the good people," said Dr. King.

Stand by your convictions. Summon the courage to be uncommon.

KEYS FOR DEVELOPING YOUR CORE

1. Remember that what you do when no one is watching matters.
2. The means matter as much as the ends, if not more.
3. Hang in there. Character is revealed through adversity.
4. Often we grow as much through the little things as we do through the big ones.
5. Truth is critical. Being truthful is too.
6. Don't rationalize your way around honesty.

7. Don't blow your own horn.

8. Don't be falsely modest; you have amazing gifts. Just recognize that others do too.

9. You are important, but not indispensable. The same goes for others. See yourself as a significant part of the process.

10. Be careful what you do with your resources, gifts, time, and talents. You've been entrusted with them.

11. Some of the most rewarding times in life are when you have to stand alone, even if you are uncomfortable doing so.

12. Life is hard. Courage is essential.

13. Never give up. Never.

PART II

LOVE
YOUR FAMILY

+ + +

Be who you are and say
what you feel, because
those who mind don't
matter and those who
matter don't mind.

DR. SEUSS

CHAPTER 5

HOW TO TREAT A WOMAN

I first learned the concept of nonviolence in my marriage.
    MOHANDAS GANDHI

THE WAY YOU TREAT WOMEN will impact every other area of your life at some point.

It will stretch beyond your immediate relationships with your wife or girlfriend to your friends, parents, and children. Character is revealed in the way you treat others and how you handle these relationships.

Your Present Role: Tough, Timid, or Something Else

I wish this were obvious; it feels like it should be. However, many guys I have known fall into one camp or the other— they either flex their muscles around women (figuratively, usually) or become completely passive. Not all guys, but many. Neither is the right approach. It's hard to blame our young men, though. Today's generation hasn't had the best teachers, because many of our dads either weren't around or somehow didn't show us how to truly love a woman. And TV and movies usually focus on erotic love, not emotional, spiritual love.

Some guys are so bent on being tough—or at least acting tough—that when respect doesn't seem to flow their way naturally, they *demand* it, holding it over everyone around them, including their wives. And Christian men are no exception; all too often, we are even worse. Completely confused by the tension between societal values and what we believe to be set out in Scripture, we either fall back on the "head of household" concept as an excuse to take control, or we think Christ requires that we become passive and weak. Because of this, we either reject a real relationship with Jesus (understandable, since who wants to go through life as a doormat?) or we crumble and abandon our proper roles in our families and in the rest of our relationships.

Christ exhibited a great number of qualities—He was sinless, loving, compassionate, and athletic (people in Jesus' time walked everywhere, remember, and He was a carpenter!), to name a few. I don't think "nice" would make the list, though, and I am certain that "passive" wouldn't either.

According to 1 Corinthians 13, love means doing everything for someone else's benefit. Of course, this *doesn't* mean giving in to that person's every wish or desire, but it does mean making every decision with his or her well-being in mind.

Love means being active in the life of your family. Take your family to church. Attend school conferences and get to know your children's teachers. Occasionally take your kids to school or pick them up. Talk to them, and more importantly, listen to them. Sit with them. Play with them on their turf—find out what interests them. Be involved.

In case you think I've strayed into another topic, this really is all about how you treat women. Yes, we need to honor women with respect in direct, one-on-one ways such as speaking and acting gentlemanly toward them—holding doors and otherwise considering their needs—but there are also indirect ways by which we can show respect. Nurturing your family also honors your wife.

A few years back, during a press conference preceding a playoff game, a reporter asked me what I had done Friday afternoon to prepare—presumably for the game. But Friday afternoons during the season have always been personal time for us as a staff. I learned from Chuck Noll that you don't change your schedule just because it's a playoff game. So because we finished early on Friday, I went home and cleaned the house. Lauren had been out of town and was due back that evening, so I wanted her to come home to a clean house. This was something I could do to aid her well-being, and at that time it was a better gift than taking her out or buying her an expensive piece of jewelry. When I told the reporter how I had spent my time, he laughed at what he thought was a joke. But I was serious. "I cleaned the house," I repeated.

I try to find ways that I can chip in to make our house a sanctuary for Lauren. I learned that from my dad, who would give my mom some space and time to herself by taking us kids out to a park or otherwise keeping us occupied for an afternoon. This gave Mom a chance to go off and shop or whatever—something just for her. As much as he enjoyed doing things with her, he knew that giving her the gift of time—away from us—was just as important.

But he also made sure there were times that we *all* did things together as a family, he and my mom included. That was important for two reasons: first, he was making memories with all of us as a family unit, and second, he was modeling his behavior toward my mom in front of us. We didn't realize it at the time, but it left a deep impression upon all of us. My brother and I were able to see how to honor and respect a woman. My two sisters were developing a point of reference for qualities they should look for in a husband. How many girls settle for substandard relationships because they don't have that frame of reference?

My dad was never passive in how he modeled Christ for us around the house. Passiveness wasn't what we learned from him. Too many men are continually baffled by their wives or can't figure out how to interact with their families. There are countless books on how women think, so I'll leave it at this: they are different. That much I've figured out. They are not men. I know that seems ridiculously obvious, but we can't approach them as we would one of the guys. So how do we do it? Be involved with them—without bringing our own agendas. Again, do everything for the *benefit* of your loved one. Without being involved—deeply involved—with Lauren for all these years and trying to listen to not only her words but also her heart, I wouldn't have made any progress at all. We've invested time in our marriage. We've talked in the evenings about finances and children. We've gone on dates. And as much as possible, I've tried to create an environment on her terms. The interesting and blessed thing about that is this: she's tried to do the same for me.

The All Pro Dad organization gives away shirts that state the "Ten Ways to Be an All Pro Dad." Number one? Love your wife. And the most important way to show that love to your wife is to be involved: as a leader, listener, and encourager. Lead by helping with discipline, setting curfews and ground rules for the television and other technology use. Lead by being in unity with your wife. And listen—not to solve the problems of the day, as so often we will try to do. Just listen so she knows you care. She's smart enough to solve her own problems, but she may appreciate your input even more if it's offered at an appropriate time—later. In the meantime, tell her you love her, offer encouragement for something she's tried or wants to try, and hold her every time she comes close. Be there for her.

Loving the woman in your life follows the same principle of the old county-fair raffle rules: must be present to win.

A God-Ordained Partnership

There is a lot of talk in church circles about the role of men and women in marriage. What concerns me is that these discussions tend to focus on who gets to be in charge. But the Bible makes it clear that both husbands and wives are supposed to be looking out for each others' well-being, not concentrating on who has the power. That means, as a husband, I'm supposed to be doing everything for the good of my wife.

Look at it another way. If God is our Father, that means He is our wives' Father too. God is my Father-in-law. That's pretty heavy.

Maybe we need to start here. Take a look in the mirror and recall all the things you are good at—in your career, at home, with the children, at church, and around the neighborhood. Then think about the things that you love to do—those things that you are passionate about. How about those things you're not so good at or that you never look forward to doing?

Now take a quiet moment to do the same for your wife. What is she really good at? What does she love to do? What would she be good at doing if she had the opportunity to give it a try?

If you are completely honest, you will begin to see that you are each gifted differently and that you each have passions—some of which are similar, but many of which are different. The saying that "opposites attract" is not always true in relationships, but I must admit that Lauren and I are as different as night and day in a lot of things. There's a simple explanation for this: we are each uniquely created, like no one else anywhere—no one. And God brought us together to complement each other. We have each been given unique insights, passions, experiences, and wisdom—for the benefit of this relationship, for each other, and even for those beyond our immediate family. I wonder if God had that in mind when we stood before each other at the altar. Each of us brings what He has created within us to this relationship, for this particular time, for the benefit of each other, our marriage, and all we will impact together through our marriage: children, friends, and others.

It seems as if the obvious conclusion is that this was a relationship made in heaven, a partnership of the highest order. Two people uniquely made and gifted for the benefit of each other and our relationship.

What about your marriage relationship? What decisions or tasks do you face together? Will one of you be more equipped to take the lead in some of those tasks? There's nothing wrong with a division of labor. We don't ask the linemen to throw the ball or the quarterbacks to block (very often). How will you decide together who will undertake what task—for the benefit of each other and the marriage? Will each person have the opportunity for input? Will you respect one another's gifts, abilities, wisdom, intuition, and insights? Are you willing to help in an area that is "her" responsibility in order to tangibly show your love for her? Those are the questions we as men need to answer to ensure the emotional well-being of our wives and allow our marriage relationship to maximize the talents of each partner.

Not unlike a team . . . just one clearly made in heaven.

An Excited Utterance or a Solemn Vow

This will require a step back in time, perhaps even a dusting off of some cobwebs. It may be a long-ago moment remembered only once a year on an anniversary, or it may be one still etched firmly in your mind.

Take a look back to that moment at the altar when you both exchanged the vows of marriage, filled with all the excitement and high-sounding promises of the fairy-tale journey you were beginning together. That excitement overshadowed all the difficult moments, valleys, and mountains you would face together in the years to come.

The best I can remember—and I probably need to remember more often—was that John Guest, the minister who married us, asked me the first question:

"Tony, will you have Lauren to be your wedded wife, to live together in the holy state of matrimony? Will you love her, comfort her, honor, and keep her in sickness and in health; and forsaking all others, keep you only unto her so long as you both shall live?"

My response—I do remember this—was "I will."

Then Lauren was given the same opportunity to stay at the altar . . . or run.

A moment later, I made this eternal commitment out loud before Lauren, God, and all assembled:

"I, Tony, take you, Lauren, to be my wedded wife, to have and to hold from this day forward, for better, for worse, for richer, for poorer, in sickness and in health, to love and to cherish, till death do us part, according to God's holy ordinance. This is my solemn vow."

I remember Lauren then making the same commitment to me.

I suspect many of you made the same commitments to each other not too long—or maybe very long—ago. The question is this: Do those commitments carry the weight in your relationship today that they were meant to, or does your marriage indicate that they were just fluff and show, words spoken only in the emotion of the moment?

Once again, the answer to that question is the difference between being common and uncommon. Common knowledge today says that this vow is just a tradition. It really doesn't mean what it says: we will try this relationship out, and as long as my wife is doing everything I expect, the way I think it should be done, I'll show her love and respect. But if she somehow doesn't meet my expectations, then I can move on and look for someone who does. We can chalk it up to "irreconcilable differences."

Christ, on the other hand, encourages the uncommon approach: what God has joined together let no man separate. I have a duty to make this marriage work, to be a man of my word.

Keep in mind, sometimes the better comes *after* the worse. Hang in there.

If your experiences are anything like mine, you and your spouse have gone through a lot since you made your vows. When times get tough, how often do we return to that moment to help us get through them?

Or perhaps it would help to go even further back to an even more miraculous moment. The first time I read John 3:16 with Lauren in mind, the realization of its meaning hit me right between the eyes.

> *"For God so loved the world that He gave His one and only Son . . ."*

Read it again:

> *"For God so loved* Lauren *that He gave His one and only Son . . ."*

The implications of this verse should move you, as it has moved me, to pray for forgiveness. Forgiveness for all the moments I missed enjoying the uniqueness of her creation. Forgiveness for all the times I missed out on her laughter, tenderness, acceptance—missed as a result of my self-centeredness.

When things are not going as smoothly as I wish, this passage has moved me to pray that God would change not her, but me. Perhaps it will move you in the same way. God loves your spouse and values her—just as she is, just as He created her—and demonstrated His love for her by sending His Son. Perhaps it will move you to change your heart to accept all of her—with all her radiant beauty, grace, and differences.

I suspect you will begin to sense an answer to your prayer through the smile that begins to form on your face, the laughter that creases your eyes, and the warm appreciation that begins to swell in your heart for the one He joined you with so long ago at that altar.

Remember, what began as excitement and exuberance ultimately became a solemn vow before God.

Picking a Partner

Perhaps you aren't married yet. Take your time. Pray that God will show you who it will be. It is one of the most important decisions of your adult life. It will impact everything in your future: your family, your finances, your career, your retirement. And to the women reading this, don't settle for substandard. You deserve a loving and caring husband. Be patient, and you'll find the one God has created for you.

The Bible says that we are not to be unequally yoked,[4] invoking the metaphor of oxen yoked together to pull a plow. The obvious implication is that if the oxen do not work well together, they won't pull in straight lines and therefore won't be productive. It's an uncomfortable place to be if you're attached at the shoulder.

I think this verse cuts to the heart of the issue: you're to find someone whose basic philosophy of life is the same as yours. In short, is her faith coming from the same source as yours? Are her values?

Beyond that, however, God has a marvelous ability to complement our lives with partners who can make them that much more complete. That is, I don't think it matters that

---

[4] See 2 Corinthians 6:14–16.

she's a Republican and you're a Democrat, or that you see eye to eye on all other issues of the day. I have even heard of instances—albeit rare—in which Colts and Patriots fans have been blissfully married. Anything is possible if *real* love is at the heart of it, and the fabric of our lives often can be richer for it.

CHAPTER 6

FATHERHOOD

One father is more than a hundred schoolmasters.
    OLD ENGLISH PROVERB

FATHERHOOD IS NOTHING IF NOT an adventure.

William Wordsworth described fatherhood in the highest of terms: "Father!—to God himself we cannot give a holier name." On the flip side, one of my favorite dads, Bill Cosby, has a slightly more earthly view of things: "Fatherhood is pretending the present you love most is soap-on-a-rope."

Both are right.

And today fatherhood remains one of the critical foundations for the health of our current generation and for those that will follow. The way fatherhood is viewed in the future is in large part dependent upon the way that today's fathers, grandfathers, and father figures handle the responsibilities of this role that has been entrusted to them.

Being Present

I'm worried about the vacuum we've left in this country with the ever-growing problem of absentee fathers. It seems that it has almost become perfectly acceptable to not be a part of your child's life as long as you meet your financial responsibilities. This would be fine, I suppose, if child support was what defined fatherhood. I worry that we've forgotten what it means to nurture our children, believing that as long as we provide financial support, the mothers of our children can provide whatever emotional growth our children need. I strongly disagree.

Strongly.

I know not all of you are fathers, but to those of you who are, I have one request: Be there for your children! Too many young men and boys are growing up without a male role model in the house to show them what it means to be a man.

There are so many reasons beyond financial support for us to be present—really *there* physically and emotionally—in the lives of our children. Studies have shown that the father's relationship with his daughter will be the primary predictor in the success of her marriage, relationships with men, and her sexual behavior prior to marriage. In particular, the research shows that if she isn't treated well by her father, or has no father in the home to nurture her, love her, and make her feel secure, she will attempt to fill that void through relationships with other men. As for our sons, if there is no father to model proper behavior for them, they will never learn what it means to be a man or a father.

Yet even for those of us fathers who are in the home, we need to be careful not to become absentee fathers by handing our children over to television sets or other people while we attend social events, catch up with friends, pursue career advancement, and do other "important" things. Many of our children go to bed without their dad at home, or at least without one who is regularly there.

We need to realize that the boys in those homes might become fathers and the girls might become mothers, and without some intervention, they are destined to continue the dysfunctional cycle. These children are missing an important part of the emotional stimulation they need: the part they can only get from their dads.

I was fortunate, I know. My father was always a part of our lives, married to my mom until the day she died, and involved in everything his children did. And I'm trying to do the same with my children. Believe me, it's difficult. As much as I try, I don't think I've done as good a job as my father did.

When it comes to being present in the lives of our children, the limitations and obstacles are enormous. Some of you are divorced, while others have jobs that involve long commutes or constant travel. In any event, you may find it tough to be there every evening for dinner, to attend your children's activities, or to tuck them in at bedtime—all of which are important to the healthy development of your children.

I'm often in that situation during the football season. In fact, I coached the 2008 season in Indianapolis while my family lived in Florida, so I'm just like a lot of the parents who travel several nights a week or live apart from their families. I'm missing more time with my children than I would like.

I'm committed to making it to my son's high school football games, and my family comes up to Indianapolis for the Colts' games, but otherwise, I don't see much of them during the Colts' season. I watched my father do this for years. He took a job teaching at Delta College in Saginaw, Michigan, but we wanted to finish high school in Jackson. He decided he would sacrifice to make it work, and I'm finding out now what a big sacrifice that was. Through it all, however, my dad remained actively involved in the household and was unified with my mom in raising us. He also spent a lot of time driving to events that were important to us. And before that, he had spent a lot of time with us, letting us know we were his number one priority. That's what made it easier for us to accept the times that he wasn't there.

Every year since 1984, when our first daughter, Tiara, was born, I have tried to figure out, given the time demands on NFL coaches, how I could maximize my family time. When I went to work for the Kansas City Chiefs in 1989, the work hours increased even more. One of the things I decided to give up was golf. Although I enjoyed playing, I was never very good at it, and we had such limited time off in Kansas City that I couldn't justify not being home when I got the chance. I've never really picked it back up, and I'm sure if I did, my game wouldn't be pretty anyway. Maybe, however, if one of our younger children takes up the game and needs a playing partner or a caddy—we'll just have to see.

When I lived full-time in Tampa, I always drove my children to school. In fact, I've even driven the neighbor children to school. Some of these trips, of course, came after a late road game, and other parents would look at me strangely, wordlessly saying, "Didn't I see you in San Diego last night on TV?" But I have always believed that as my children's father and Lauren's husband, I was responsible for driving the children to school.

So, whether we won or lost, regardless of how tired I was—or even if I had been fired the day before—I drove the carpool. (And yes, I did drive the morning after I was fired!)

I became aware of how much my job impacted our kids when they stopped wanting to go out with me in public, even to the mall, the movies, or to dinner. They got tired of the fact that we were always stopping to talk to people who recognized me. I realized then that my job already takes a lot of family time away from them—either because I have to be gone so much or because we are often interrupted when we are out in public. Because our time is so limited, it's even more precious—to them and to me.

I will continue to evaluate the time I spend with my family every year as long as we have children under our roof, I'm certain. I have to—for their sakes and mine.

What You Say and Do

Just because you've erred doesn't mean you're out of the running to be a good dad. The Bible wasn't written for those who have it figured out, but instead it is God's Word to those of us who are muddling through life. We must remember that "all have sinned and fall short of the glory of God,"[5] but we have been given the freedom through Christ to forget the past and look forward to what lies ahead as we "press on to reach the end of the race."[6]

If you thought I was going to share what I feel is important about fatherhood because I'm an expert on how it should be done correctly, you can see that I'm not. However, if you're willing to listen to the things I think I have done right and

[5] Romans 3:23, NIV
[6] Philippians 3:13-14

learn from the mistakes I've made and am working to correct, then keep reading.

We've all come up short. That doesn't mean that you can't gather yourself, draw a line of new commitment in the sand, and move on.

Here's something to think about: How do you speak to your children? What we say is terribly important. I've put this concept in this section because our children are so emotionally dependent on us, but it could just as easily be in the section on loving our wives (how many women are subjected to emotional and verbal abuse by husbands who wouldn't dream of physically striking them?) or on dealing with friends, coworkers, and others whom we influence.

Words are powerful, as noted by many through the ages. James 3:3-6 says this:

> *We can make a large horse go wherever we want by means of a small bit in its mouth. And a small rudder makes a huge ship turn wherever the pilot chooses to go, even though the winds are strong. In the same way, the tongue is a small thing that makes grand speeches. But a tiny spark can set a great forest on fire. And the tongue is a flame of fire. It is a whole world of wickedness, corrupting your entire body. It can set your whole life on fire.*

Similarly, Ralph Waldo Emerson noted the power—both good and bad—of our words:

> *No man has a prosperity so high or firm, but that two or three words can dishearten it; and there is no calamity which right words will not begin to redress.*

Our words can uplift and heal and empower—or not. Words can inspire, rekindle a sense of wonder, and provide direction, or they can dampen spirits, condemn ideas, and destroy initiative. We've all seen examples of this. Words can be used to delight and provide comfort—especially needed in the case of our children. Just know that your children are always looking for affirmation, for the knowledge that they matter—to *you*—even when their behavior would indicate otherwise. Words can bring peace to a family, they can restore a soul, they can certainly instruct and provide counsel, and they can encourage the downtrodden, strengthen the weak, and lift those who have fallen.

If the moments around our families are filled with peaceful, soothing, and uplifting conversations, some of us may fall into believing that this doesn't apply to us. But let me caution you on this. Just because your body is in the house, it doesn't mean that you are *there*. Your children need *you* to affirm and encourage them. Even if you are fighting workaholic tendencies, make sure you communicate openly and lovingly with your family. Since I wasn't even in the same state as my family during the 2008 season, I needed to be intentional about picking up the phone and talking with my children regularly. Be intentional with your words.

Jim Caldwell, one of the men who has coached alongside me both in Tampa Bay and Indianapolis, began writing cards to his daughter when she left home to attend college. She was in South Carolina playing basketball, and Jim was in Indiana coaching football, so their times together were very limited, and even telephone calls were sporadic. But as Jim tells it, Natalie knew that if she was in a pinch because she had overspent her allowance that month, Dad was the easy target. Being much wiser than many men I have known, Jim sent the money, but he also used that opportunity to write his daughter a note of encouragement or affirmation.

"I always stuck it in a card, because I wasn't sure how much mail she received," he said. "I never kidded myself that I had anything particularly profound to say in the cards, or that she even was looking to get cards from me.

"We traveled down there her sophomore year and visited her apartment. On the living room wall, taped in a row at eye level, were all of the cards I'd sent during her college days.

"All of a sudden I realized that I hadn't written her nearly enough."

They're Watching, Too

In addition to looking for opportunities to lift your children up with your words, great care should be taken in watching what you do. Your children are more observant and perceptive than you may think.

What we say as fathers is important, but not nearly as much as what we do. Our children are smart—they will notice if we are living lives that are inconsistent with what we're saying and teaching.

Those of you with children have no doubt witnessed their amazing inclination toward mimicry. For those of you who have yet to be blessed with children of your own or who haven't had many occasions to be around them, trust me when I tell you that Rodney Atkins has captured the truth of this fact and the role and responsibility of a father in his song "Watching You." The father is tucking his son in for the night, and the small boy spontaneously and confidently says his prayers. The surprised father asks the boy where he learned to pray like that:

> He said, "I've been a-watching you, Dad, ain't that cool?
> I'm your buckaroo, I wanna be like you. . . .
> I wanna do everything you do
> So I've been watching you."

This was recently brought home to me by my seven-year-old, Jordan. Whenever something goes wrong, either on the football field or at home, the first words that come out of my mouth are, "You've *got* to be kidding me!" Well, not too long ago, when two-year-old Justin broke one of Jordan's favorite toys, Jordan's first response was, "You've *got* to be kidding me!" and he even put just the right emphasis on the word *got*!

Our children are watching; there's no doubt about it. If you tell your son that it's important to treat women well and then don't demonstrate that in your actions toward your wife, he will get the real message of what you believe. Or when you teach honesty as an abstract point, and then voluntarily tell the cashier that she gave you too much change and hand money back to her, your children will see that, too. If they see that work and status—above your family—are what drives you as a man, then no matter what you say and how many times you say it, they will learn to value those things as well.

Words Optional

Even in light of the great importance of speaking affirming words to our children, sometimes the best thing we can do as parents is to be quiet. Our children need to know that we're always there for them, no matter what.

And as we're walking through all of these ups and downs as fathers, we need to remember that God loves us. No matter what we've done or where we've been, He's there to embrace us, with all the muck we're in and mess we've made. That's our model of fatherhood. Not the flawed or absent models from our childhood, but a loving God who stands ready to gather us into His arms. And that's what we want our children to know—that God loves them. They will see it first modeled by us.

Yes, we will no doubt fall short, but for the sake of our children—and their children and their children's children—we need to strive to reflect the love that is daily demonstrated by our God.

In the 1992 Summer Olympics in Barcelona, Spain, Derek Redmond believed he could win a silver medal for Great Britain. After five years of daily training and eight operations on his Achilles tendons, Derek had won the first two heats and was running in the semifinals of the 400 meters. Things were going as planned until, coming out of the first turn, he heard a snap and felt a sharp pain in his left leg. Derek went down in a heap on the track as he realized that his left hamstring had exploded, and with it, his dreams of an Olympic medal.

He got to his feet and began to run—hop, really—to finish the race. He later said that he was determined to finish and therefore waved off the race officials, who were running toward him with a stretcher.

And then he felt a hand on his shoulder.

Redmond began to push the hand of assistance away until he turned to find himself looking into the face of his father, Jim. When Jim Redmond had seen what had happened to his son, he had pushed his way out of the crowd and onto the track and rushed to tell Derek that he didn't have to finish. But when Derek insisted that he complete the race, Jim said they would do it together.

Derek cried into Jim's shoulder as they walked the remainder of the course, and race officials continued to come to their side in an effort to assist the pair. Jim now was the one who waved them off, later saying he didn't understand Spanish, and wasn't going to be stopped from being with his son.

Our children need to know that we're there to help them pick up the pieces of their shattered dreams, to tell them that they're okay, to help them see that failure isn't final, and that when they take their next steps, they will not be alone. Quality time is important. Being actively engaged with our children in their schoolwork or their activities or by simply reading a book is important. But they need *quantity* time, too, and lots of it. Even if there's nothing special on the agenda, they need to know that we've chosen to be in the room or in the house with them, over all the other interests competing for our time.

Sacred Trusts—Sacred Memories

Here's something I want you to think about in the days ahead.

When was the last time you did something really silly with or in front of your children? When was the last time you did something totally unexpected and spontaneous that your children remember to this day? Like jumping in the swimming pool with your clothes on, or "accidentally" spraying whipped cream all over your face, starting a pillow fight in the bedroom, or splashing in the puddles after a summer rain?

When was the last time you set aside all the "important" things you had to do and followed your children to wherever they wanted you to go? Have they asked you to do something recently? Maybe you've said no so many times that they don't bother to ask anymore. I hope that's not the case.

Think about this: How many more of those moments will you have? How long will it be before other interests and demands on your children's lives preempt the opportunities for you to do things together, to listen to their hearts as you spend the day together, and to talk about the things they need to know—like how wonderfully they have been created?

Since my oldest son's death in 2005, I have talked to hundreds of parents who have lost children to accidents, illness, or violence. Every one of those parents, including me, wishes they could spend a few more minutes with their child, doing something fun together. The Bible says that tomorrow is not promised to us. We need to take advantage of the opportunities we have today. Life is what happens when we're making other plans.

How long will it be before the playroom—and most of the other rooms in your house as well—will be neat, tidy, and in perfect order, noticeably devoid of the laughing and chattering personalities of God's little angels? Will the walls of those once sacred places be filled with regrets, or with wonderful memories? Will you see the fingerprints of God in every nook and cranny from His precious little messengers, or will you see only a memorial of might-have-beens?

Trent Dilfer, who was drafted by the Buccaneers two years before I was hired as the head coach, is a terrific man and father. In 2003, after we had both moved on from the Bucs, Trent's son, Trevin, was stricken with something that appeared to be the flu while they were at Disneyland. He was only five, and Trent and his wife, Cass, never anticipated that Trevin's heart was being attacked by a virus.

Despite the best care that he could get at Stanford University, Trevin died six weeks later, with his mom, dad, and three sisters by his side. We ached for Trent. At the time, I didn't know how he could handle himself so well in light of his loss. When I asked, Trent attributed it to his faith. Little did I know that my family would be clinging to that same faith when faced with our own agony just two short years later.

I don't know what's going on in your life right now. I don't know what important stuff you have in front of you. I don't know what or who is bothering you or trying to set your schedule for tomorrow or days ahead. But I wonder if we all need to do a better job of listening to that gentle whisper from a God who daily reminds us to enjoy the sacred moments with those we love—with dear friends, with those who need us, and especially with our precious children. They are moments we will look back on with either regret or a smile.

Either way, the memory will last forever.

CHAPTER 7

RESPECT AUTHORITY

When I was a boy of fourteen, my father was so ignorant I could hardly stand to have the old man around. But when I got to be twenty-one, I was astonished at how much he had learned in seven years.

Mark Twain

MY FATHER WAS A NOTORIOUS bargain hunter. He believed in the value of a dollar and didn't like to overspend on anything. I didn't always appreciate those lessons, especially when it came to buying something for me. I remember one of those times quite clearly. I was in the seventh grade and had outgrown my old bike. My dad knew how much I wanted a new bike, and I could tell that it was important to him that we find one.

It wasn't an easy process.

We must have visited eight different bike stores. We started out in a store in our hometown of Jackson, Michigan, and then moved outward in a journey of concentric circles to those in Ann Arbor and then Detroit. We couldn't research things online in those days, so more legwork was involved—and a lot more time! And boy, did we use legwork, when all I wanted was a new bike. Now!

I tried to convince my dad that the gas we were using would make up for any savings he might realize, but he disagreed. I didn't appreciate where he was coming from until later, when the lessons of that extensive investigative journey sank in: the value of a dollar, the importance of a deliberate process, and the rewards of deferred gratification.

Not everything that my father did made sense to me as a boy, but I learned at an early age that I should respect him and that I could trust his authority as my father, whether or not I agreed with him. It will come as no surprise to you that at the time, his decisions and the consequences he sometimes imposed did not always seem fair to me. But as I got older, it became increasingly clear that my best interests and those of my brother and sisters were paramount to my parents, and they expected us to honor them and the decisions they made for our lives.

My parents also made it very clear that this was rooted in God's Word. The Bible was their guide, and because we were being raised on biblical principles, there were some things that were just going to be done a certain way, whether we liked it or not. We were to honor them as the Bible commanded,[7] through our obedience and respect. I could disagree with them, and often did, but I had to accept their decisions and learn to deal with them.

---

[7] "Honor your father and mother. Then you will live a long, full life in the land the LORD your God is giving you" (Exodus 20:12).

Others in Authority

Our parents aren't the only source of authority in our lives, however. God has placed others over us as well, as I have been reminded repeatedly in life, particularly while I was the head coach of the Tampa Bay Buccaneers. In two notable instances, I knew in my heart that I should defer to authority, and I had the benefit of good counsel to help with my decisions. In *Quiet Strength*, I wrote of a time when the Bucs' owners felt changes were needed on our staff and asked me to remove Mike Shula from his position as offensive coordinator. Mike was not only a good friend, but he had also done exactly what I wanted him to do in his role, so I agonized over this dilemma.

I talked with my pastor, Ken Whitten, about the situation, and he shared a great deal of wisdom with me. In Romans 13:1-2, Paul told the early church in Rome that they must obey even the Roman rulers:

> *Everyone must submit to governing authorities. For all*
> *authority comes from God, and those in positions of*
> *authority have been placed there by God. So anyone who*
> *rebels against authority is rebelling against what God has*
> *instituted, and they will be punished.*

Remember, though, that the apostle Paul didn't say this only as a recognition of the role of the government in protecting and serving its citizens. He was also hoping that, by submitting to the governing authorities, early Christians could keep the peace as much as possible and allow the continued spread of the gospel. Of course, if the government or any governing authorities abuse that power, they will be accountable to God. In that regard, I do believe that there are exceptions to this scriptural admonition concerning submission to governing authorities, but I was pretty sure this wasn't one of those situations. After much thought, I came to the conclusion that God had placed me under the authority of the Glazer family, who owned the Bucs, and that what they were asking me to do wasn't illegal or immoral or contrary to my loyalty, relationship, or allegiance to God.

As painful as it was for me, and as much as I disagreed with the decision, I felt I had no choice but to fire Mike.

The second instance occurred when the Glazers fired me. Lauren and I were obviously very disappointed and hurt by the decision, but the night it happened, we sat down with my friend Tom Lamphere, who is the Minnesota Vikings' chaplain, and he helped us understand that it's not always easy to submit to authority.

We talked about what I should say at the press conference the following day, and he encouraged me not to lash out at the Glazers. This was good advice. That press conference actually turned out to be a moment of healing for me and my family—and, I believe, for the community as well.

At that press conference, we were able to focus on the positive elements of our time in Tampa: the lessons we had learned there and the memories we would take away—in no small part attributable to a lifetime of learning to accept authority. Was I disappointed and displeased? Was it disruptive to our family? Sure, but there are times when decisions are made that we disagree with but must live with, and over time, we realize that life goes on.

The Influence of Your Authority

We all have positions of authority—often many and varied. And in those positions of authority, we must always be aware of the influence we have on others. Many of us are coaches—maybe of professional or college football teams or high school or youth soccer teams. Still others have positions of influence in our work or community activities, with neighborhood groups, friends, or those whom we have never even met and perhaps never will.

I always marvel at the unexpected—and undeserved—influence that I am able to have on people, and I try to never underestimate that potential for impact. My son Eric plays wide receiver on his high school team. Like the dad that I am, I have long been concerned with him getting a well-rounded start to his day.

"Make sure you eat a good breakfast," I've told him time and again. "Froot Loops are not what I'm talking about." He listens but likes his Froot Loops.

Recently, Eric changed schools, and on the second day of school, he attended an introductory meeting of the football team. He came in to talk to me before bed that night.

"Dad, we're going to need to leave earlier for school tomorrow."

"Sure, what's up?"

"Coach told us that we really need to be taking care of our bodies, and that starts with getting a good breakfast. The only thing we have here is Froot Loops, so we'll need to go early enough so that we can stop somewhere for something more nutritious."

Don't ever underestimate your authority or influence.

Patience with Your Parents

In 2005, our son Jamie took his life for reasons that we'll never understand. During the days that followed, my daughter Tiara made an observation that has stuck with me ever since: "I just wish he could have made it until he was twenty, because when I was seventeen or eighteen, sometimes the things that you guys say to us just didn't make sense. But when I got to twenty, those things started making sense again. I just wish he would have made it to twenty."

Children, be patient with your parents (even those of you who are grown children). We are doing the best we can, and we don't always make the right decisions or say the right things. Just know this: we love you and want what's best for you.

As I told those who had gathered during Jamie's home-going service, "And for you kids—I know there are a number of you here today who are thirteen, fourteen, fifteen—maybe your parents are starting to seem a little old-fashioned, and maybe they won't let you do some of the things you want to do. Just know, when that happens, that they still love you and care about you very much. And those old-fashioned things will start making sense pretty soon."

Be patient.

When You Can't Honor Your Father and Mother

I realize that you may have a hard time with this whole idea of honoring your parents and respecting authority. I realize that you may not have had the benefit of the loving, nurturing, and dedicated parents that I was blessed with.

Maybe you had a less-than-desirable childhood. Maybe you came from a broken home. Maybe you had a parent who left and never darkened your door again, leaving a void you still feel today. Maybe you were abused—physically, emotionally, or otherwise—and along with the scars of abuse, there remains a bitterness you can't seem to get beyond. Maybe you don't want to let it go; perhaps you feel that you have the right to be angry for what was done to you. Perhaps you feel as if what you experienced was somehow your fault.

Maybe you've come to view yourself as unworthy, and the unfortunate, thoughtless, and hurtful actions of others have colored your idea of what you can expect from your heavenly Father.

You don't want that to be the story for the rest of your life!

You may need to seek professional help or talk to a pastor or trusted friend. But somehow you need to get to a place of healing and wholeness. Whether you realize it or not, God created you with unique gifts and abilities, and He has given you a unique purpose. He wants to use you for extraordinary accomplishments. But, sadly, those gifts and abilities haven't been fully tapped, and the real purpose of the journey of your life hasn't really begun, all because of something that you had no control over. Days and years of your life have passed by while you looked for help and relief from everything you were feeling. You may not have known where to turn for relief, so you tried to find it by immersing yourself in careers, alcohol, drugs, or relationships.

While you've been searching for satisfaction and a sense of fulfillment, you may not have even realized that the God who created you is still there and loves you with an unconditional and never-ending love. You may have never experienced this kind of unconditional love from your parents. You may have never received the blessing from your parents that we all need for that sense of affirmation and wholeness in our lives. And you may never receive it from them.

But somehow you need to be able to move on into all the fullness of life that God intended for you to live. You—with the help of others—need to forgive the people who did these things to you. You and I both know that unresolved bitterness affects *us* more than it does the one we're bitter toward. It ties us down and holds us back from becoming all we were created to be.

God loves you, in spite of the mistakes, failures, and shortcomings in your life. His love is unconditional. It never ends, and He never leaves.

I suspect that may be hard to swallow if the very ones who were supposed to love and protect you were the ones who hurt you the most. But it's true. The God who created you *will never leave you* and *will always love you.*

He stands ready to walk with you for the rest of your life; He will help you draw a line between your past and your future, and He will help you to forgive and move out into all the fullness and freedom of a brand new day. He might even help you get to a place with your parents—either in person or in your heart—where you can not only let go of the pain but also begin to honor them by giving them the blessing of your love.

Big step? Huge! But it's possible if you do it with the prayer and help of friends and family who love you now, if you get professional help where needed, and if you lean on the God who will never leave you. Remember: no one will ever love you the way that Jesus loves you. He was with you when you were born, and He is with you now.

✝   ✝   ✝

KEYS FOR LOVING YOUR FAMILY

1. Be a leader around your home, but lead for the benefit of your wife and children, not for your own benefit.
2. Give your wife breaks from her daily responsibilities.
3. Make memories.
4. Keep your vows sacred. Sometimes better comes *after* worse.
5. If you are not married, be careful in selecting a spouse. It is one of the most important decisions you will ever make.
6. Be present with your family—emotionally and physically.
7. Be careful what you say and do.
8. Write notes to your children.
9. Honor those in authority over you.
10. Be careful with the authority and influence that you've been entrusted with.
11. If you can't come to grips with your parents and your past, find a professional to walk with you through it.

PART III

LIFT
YOUR FRIENDS
& OTHERS

+ + +

Whenever you're in conflict with someone, there is one factor that can make the difference between damaging your relationship and deepening it. That factor is attitude.

WILLIAM JAMES

CHAPTER 8

FRIENDSHIP

No love, no friendship, can cross the path of our destiny without leaving some mark on it forever.
François Mauriac

CHOOSE YOUR FRIENDS for the sake of friendship.

It seems like such an obvious statement, but my parents used to say it to us all the time. Don't choose friends because they are popular, or because they are good-looking, or because they are rich or athletic. Choose your friends because you enjoy them and because they are good people.

I still miss Jamie. I'm sure I always will. One of the best lessons Jamie taught me had to do with choosing friends. He was never concerned with a person's status. In fact, the lesser someone's status, the better chance that person had of hanging out with Jamie and being brought home. The best way to become Jamie's friend was to look like you needed a friend, which reminds me of the Dale Carnegie quote that you'll make more friends in two weeks if you genuinely show interest in them than you'll have in two years if you try to get them interested in you.

Remember, friendship runs two ways. Too often, we evaluate a friendship based on the way it benefits *us*. But lasting friendships are formed when we can cause those benefits to flow toward someone else. What benefits do you bring to your friendships?

I'm not sure how well we do with that. We seem so quick to categorize others, so quick to determine people's worth based on what they can do for us, where they live, what they drive or wear, or what their occupation is. It's been my experience that we value NFL coaches far more than we should, and nurses and teachers not nearly enough.

Choose your friends for the sake of friendship—their friendship to you, and more importantly, your friendship to them.

Start there.

Friends for Values

Choose your friends based on their values, not their status in society.

I am grateful for that legacy from my parents; however, I probably shouldn't give them all the credit because I believe they learned it from *their* parents.

But I saw this lesson lived out every day by my folks. Within our extended family, I had a number of uncles who worked very different jobs. One was a high-ranking member of law enforcement, another was an autoworker, another was a baker, and so on. It never occurred to me that these positions might carry value; to me, each of them was my uncle—they all loved me and looked out for me, and I cared for them all. Their value, for me and others who knew them, was not determined by their job titles but by the men they were twenty-four hours a day, whether working at their jobs, or hanging out at home, or doing something else in their communities.

Similarly, when it came to choosing my friends, my parents encouraged me to hang around people who had inner cores that would build me up. I still look for this today: friends who were raised to share the same values my parents were trying to instill in me. Friends who will reinforce those values when I am with them. At the same time, my parents discouraged me from hanging around people who didn't share our values. I knew I should be friendly to them, but I shouldn't be friends with them.

Many of my current friends are coaches. Many are not. I haven't selected any of my friends based on their status, however. Instead, I look for people of character whose company I enjoy. What I value most about my friends is the way their own life choices reinforce those values that have been ingrained in me for so long by my parents and others.

I have always enjoyed attending the coaches' camps put on each year by the Fellowship of Christian Athletes. At these camps, no one cares about status. NFL head coaches interact with high school assistant coaches; Division I college coaches spend time with small school coaches. If you listened in on the conversations, you'd never know who was who—which is good, because it doesn't matter. They are just guys who share the same values and the same passions—enjoying football, helping young men, and living for Christ. Where they happen to be coaching, how often their teams play on television, or how many games they've won in the last year—those aren't the important things.

What matters is the reinforcement and reminders these men bring to me that affect so many areas of my life. We may not share the same way of doing things, but we share the same values. And for me, that short week spent together provides much-needed encouragement and recharges my batteries for when I return to the day-to-day experiences of living in a world where status is too highly valued.

Friends—Voices of Godly Wisdom and Direction

No doubt if you were asked to do so, you could come up with an exhaustive list of those people in your life that you call friends.

But the list would probably become much shorter if you listed the people you seek out when you make your most important decisions. Those whose voices and wisdom you seek when you face a crossroads in your life. Friends who will stand by and guide you when you need it. Friends who put your interests before their own.

Number one on my list of those friends is my bride of more years than she might care to remember—Lauren. Hers has been a voice of encouragement, love, character, and godly wisdom for well beyond the years of our marriage. In fact, that is one of the things that attracted me to her. Her voice has always carried messages of importance, pointing me toward what is right and what is in my best interest. Those messages have shaped my character amid the lure and glamour of a world that is constantly trying to make me detour from the path that God has set before me. There are other voices of wisdom in my life as well, friends whose counsel I often seek before making the really important decisions of my life. People who see the same direction for my life that I see—God's direction. I also have friends who will correct and admonish me when it's necessary.

Too many of us—and I have been guilty of this as well—listen to the voices of the crowd, even when we know better. Often, we do this simply because there are many voices and they are the loudest: the voices of ambition, power, wealth, revenge, greed, pleasure, self-centeredness, and appeasement. At some time in our lives, we have all succumbed to one of those voices. Men and women. Celebrities, sports figures, and "role models." Church leaders. Married couples. Politicians. Parents. We have all heard them, the voices reflecting the ways of the world:

"Go ahead; no one will ever find out."

"Who can it hurt?"

"Your job is at stake; you'd better do it."

"But, Mom, all my friends are doing it."

"Compared to what others are doing, this is nothing."

"You'll never get that promotion unless you're willing to do this."

But even while all those voices bombard us, we need to learn to listen to the quiet voices consistently speaking the truth. These voices come from our wives or our parents or our close friends, those people who have been with us in the valleys and on the mountaintops of our journeys. I can still hear some things my mom said forty years ago quite distinctly in my mind today.

And if we listen closely, we may even hear the quiet voice, the whisper, of our God—our dearest friend—pointing us toward the uncommon life that He desires from us.

CHAPTER 9

TAKING COUNSEL

'Tis great confidence in a friend to tell him your faults, greater to tell him his.
    BENJAMIN FRANKLIN

I DON'T KNOW EVERYTHING.

There have been enough people in my life through the years who have made that painfully clear to me. Therefore, I must be secure enough to say, "I don't know." In fact, I really need to be secure enough to say, "I have absolutely no idea what you're talking about."

"I don't know" is always a good answer. Especially if it is true.

"I don't know—could you please enlighten me?" is often an even better answer.

There will always be someone who knows more than you do, which is good. I strongly encourage you to find those people and take them to lunch. We can learn a lot from people who know more than we do. That's one of the things I really admired about my dad. He talked to everyone—or I should say he *listened* to everyone. Most people described him as quiet, but that's because in most conversations, he listened much more than he talked. He really felt he could learn things from other people.

To me, this is the flip side of mentoring, which we will discuss a bit later. When you are mentoring, you are intentionally reaching out to help someone behind you on the path of life. But when you are seeking counsel, you are looking for someone who is already ahead of you, someone you can learn from. Being open to learning—to being mentored—is necessary for growth but is difficult for some to master. Too often, it's a matter of ego or pride, which has a way of hindering our growth and development.

We all know people who lead you to believe that they know everything about everything. When I was in college, somebody said, "If after three weeks of class you don't know who the class jerk is, then it's you." Make sure that you don't become that person who thinks he has all the answers and isn't open to the counsel of others. I've found that this attitude is often a defense mechanism, masking feelings of insecurity or fear that you'll be exposed for your lack of knowledge.

A good coaching staff is made up of people who are willing to listen to others. If I had all the answers, there would be no point in surrounding myself with bright, creative coaches—and I'm sure the team ownership would be pleased with all the money they would save in salaries. The truth is, though, that we all need to surround ourselves with the very best, smartest, and most trustworthy people we can find. And then we need to turn them loose to do their jobs and offer the input necessary to make us the best we can be.

As a coaching staff, we meet every Monday to watch film and determine which things we can improve on as a team, and then we watch our opponent's film. Next, we come up with ideas to use our strengths most effectively that week in a game plan against our opposition. I learn a lot in those times together. There's no need for a staff, however, if I've already made up my mind about what the team should do and am not willing to listen to other ideas.

We all know people who resist change or feel threatened if someone else comes up with an appropriate plan. This kind of person acts as if no idea is a good idea unless it's *his* idea.

Don't be like that. Be open to taking counsel. After all, Proverbs tell us that "plans succeed through good counsel; don't go to war [or play a football game!] without wise advice."[8] Instead, surround yourself with the best people you can find and then empower them to do their jobs. Set the vision for the course you want to take. Recognize how significant their differing skills and abilities are to the mission of the cause, team, or organization, and allow them to use those gifts and abilities to get you there. Let them know how important their contributions are to the group's success. Seek their input, listen to them, decide on the direction, and then go there together.

It could very well make the difference between common and uncommon results.

[8] Proverbs 20:18

Constructive Conflict

Don't relish conflict, but don't fear it. Conflict is one of the most misunderstood parts of our existence. It is often unpleasant; many people try to avoid it. Others seem to thrive on the stress of it. I think some even use it to overpower others. Maybe that's why they look for opportunities to bully people.

However, conflict is best seen as an opportunity to understand our differences, since that's when conflict usually arises: when we see something differently.

When a problem does come up, think constructively. You are not attacking the other person, and hopefully he is not attacking you, either. If he is, redirect him to the problem. That is what you both should be focused on: the principle, not the person.

In this day and age, too many people resort to letting arguments become personal—name-calling, mockery, personal attacks. I suppose humans have always done it. We can't stay focused on the matter before us so we get frustrated and lash out; or we realize that our position should change but we aren't confident enough to do so. That seems to be the common approach to conflict.

Don't be like that. Be *constructive*.

Be uncommon.

Stay focused on solutions and communication. Admit when you're wrong, but stand your ground when you're right.

I have always liked the movie *Twelve Angry Men*. In the movie, Henry Fonda plays a member of a jury charged with returning a verdict in a murder trial. The evidence appears clear-cut, and the other eleven are ready to return a guilty verdict and move on with their lives. But Fonda's character is not satisfied that the evidence is conclusive and he feels the need to walk through it again, much to the dismay of the other eleven jurors. Time and time again, a vote is taken, and still he stands alone. Some of the other jurors begin to make it personal. The room becomes very tense, but Fonda's character just keeps his focus on the job they've been given to do.

He exhorts the other jurors to reexamine the evidence between each vote, and the votes begin to shift: 11–1, 10–2, 8–4, and so on. Finally, after reexamining the evidence a number of times, all of the jurors agree on a verdict of not guilty.

Standing alone. Sometimes we have to stand alone for an extended period of time. Other times, the mere act of our standing for what we believe in brings others with us, and we are no longer alone.

Either way, conflict can serve to illuminate truth or illuminate differences. In any event, it doesn't have to be feared.

CHAPTER 10

THE POWER OF POSITIVE INFLUENCE

This above all: to thine own self be true,
And it must follow, as the night the day,
Thou canst not then be false to any man.
WILLIAM SHAKESPEARE'S *HAMLET*, ACT I, SCENE III

PEER PRESSURE WORKS in both directions.

Sometimes we're so busy reacting to peer pressure that we forget we're exerting it on others.

My mother taught Shakespeare for years at Jackson High School, so even though I never had any desire to take it, I couldn't help but pick some up along the way. The quotation cited from *Hamlet* is Polonius's words to his son, Laertes, before Laertes leaves to travel abroad. It's no less true today for our young men than it was four centuries ago, or at any other time in history.

To thine own self be true. This is critically important to remember as you set out in the world. You will come into contact with people who, whether they mean to or not, will exert pressure on you to conform. However, you are also in a position to influence them—for good. You can help your friends make better decisions just by your example. But to be that good example, you must have a clear foundation of who you are.

When I was traded from the Pittsburgh Steelers to the San Francisco 49ers in 1979, a lot of things in my world changed pretty drastically. I went from playing for a Super Bowl–level team in a relatively small, blue-collar city to playing for a very poor team in a large, cosmopolitan area. At twenty-four years old, in my third year of professional football, I was venturing into a different world, one with many more temptations than I had ever experienced before.

Drug use was very prevalent in the Bay Area in the late seventies. I wondered how I would respond if someone offered them to me. I didn't want to look like some small-town kid who had no clue what the "real world" was like. Because of my athletic training, my parents' influence, and my Christian beliefs, I never really considered smoking, drinking, or using any drugs. But I must admit, I did feel out of place. And I sensed that a lot of people were looking at me as being strange.

But to thine own self be true.

I later discovered that some guys *were* looking at me— and it was having an effect on them. One of my teammates had gotten into the drug culture in San Francisco because he thought that's what pro athletes did. But because I had come from a Super Bowl team in Pittsburgh, and I didn't do drugs, it made him feel he didn't have to either. Years later, he told me that my example may have saved his life; it was a lesson in role modeling I've never forgotten.

Be Original

Becoming a positive role model starts with a look in the mirror. It may take looking *through* the mirror and back into your life to see things that happened to you for which you are still trying to compensate. Maybe your childhood wasn't all that great. Maybe your career is off track. Maybe you failed at too many things you've tried. Maybe you could have done better in some of the relationships in your life.

But you were created for a reason. It doesn't matter what you missed or how you may have messed up; the fact is that *your future is still ahead of you.* What will you do with it? What did you learn from past mistakes that might make the journey ahead better? And which of those lessons do you need to model for those around you? Every day we are faced with challenges and the temptation to conform. But God made each of us with unique gifts and characteristics, and being a positive role model starts with being ourselves. Entertainers Isaac Hayes and Bernie Mac died within days of each other in the summer of 2008. Both men had been interviewed shortly before they died, and their comments contained interesting similarities. They both said that their originality was the source of their success. Hayes said that he and other artists of his era had looked for ways to express themselves and who they were. He noted that it's the same with every generation, except that the music of the current generation is too focused on what sells rather than truly expressing the artist.

Bernie Mac was asked if he had any bitterness over the fact that it took so long for his career to become a commercial success. He didn't. "I never wanted to do it for superficial reasons—for women and money and cars and stuff like that. . . . I was my own person, I was my own man, I always thought for myself. It was no pressure on me. . . . I've never been posse, and all that. I'm a quiet storm. I like doing my thing and then when I get done I like being around people who I enjoy."[9]

Mac then went on to say that he was his own kind of comic and wasn't concerned about trying to conform to the expectations others placed on comedy. He thought this approach might have contributed to his longer road to success, but at the same time, he doubted that he would have ever reached the heights he did professionally if he hadn't blazed his own trail.

Be yourself—the self that God created.

In a Changing Culture, Some Things Should Never Change

Think for a moment about those relationships in your life that mean the most to you. They probably involve one-on-one time spent face-to-face with each other. Unfortunately, with e-mail, the Internet, texting, and online virtual communities, we may be losing—by our own choices—the opportunities to develop the most meaningful of relationships. In this world of "staying connected," I wonder if we aren't, in fact, hurting our chances of developing meaningful personal relationships.

Online communities seem to be springing up everywhere, and while having many benefits, they do give me cause for concern. Kids do not realize the permanence of posting things online or see the danger in making themselves so vulnerable

---

[9] Tavis Smiley, August 12, 2008 transcript of 2007 interview

and accessible to strangers. I do see that there are also positives, in that kids like mine, who have moved around a lot, can stay connected with their good friends regardless of where they live.

My biggest concern, however, is that in forming virtual bonds, we may be forsaking true human interaction. As we interact via bits and bytes, we run the risk of further isolating ourselves. Gone are the days of neighborhoods with front porches and kids riding their bikes to a friend's house. Now cars pull into garages and the doors close behind them.

Life was meant to be lived in community. We learn from others what it means to be a man and what it means to be involved in our families or towns. I don't mind these technological advances, but let me add a word of caution: give careful thought to your family's use of them. As I understand it, the Amish and Mennonite communities of America are not opposed to technology in general, but rather ask themselves whether each advance truly improves their quality of life.

We might be wise to do the same. We are always connected these days, via cell phones, the Internet, or other electronic devices. That's great. But I think we need to make sure we're not so connected with *everything* out there that we miss the chance to be quiet and connect with the people directly in front of us.

Because it's in those real-life connections that the power of our personal influence can have life-changing, long-lasting impact.

Encourage Others

I've seen firsthand that life is tough. Just as it helps me when people encourage and lift me up, I know that others need that as well. We should all be like Joseph of Cyprus, a member of the early church whose nickname was Barnabas, which means "son of encouragement." No doubt the apostle Paul was glad to have Barnabas join him on his missionary journeys because he offered encouragement and friendship just when Paul needed them both.

Jesus says in Matthew 7:12, "Do to others whatever you would like them to do to you. This is the essence of all that is taught in the law and the prophets."

Do you want to have a positive influence on the life of someone else? Then let me ask you a few more questions. When was the last time you went to visit someone who needed a visit? When was the last time you made a call—or wrote a letter—to someone who could use a lift in his or her life? When was the last time you had a date with your spouse or a "date night" with your little girl, who adores you? When was the last time you sent flowers to someone for no particular reason? When was the last time you did something that will forever be a positive memory in someone's life?

When was the last time you were an encourager for someone else?

No matter where you are in your life's journey, you can begin today to be very intentional about leaving a trail of positive memories in the lives of those around you. Memories they will cling to in the rough spots they face over the course of their lives. Memories that will draw them closer to you and affirm their value to you and to themselves.

Life has enough memories of the tough kind, so why not create a few fond and unforgettably good ones along the way for people you love? You won't regret it—trust me.

CHAPTER 11

MENTORING

The light which experience gives is a lantern on the stern, which
shines only on the waves behind us.
    SAMUEL TAYLOR COLERIDGE

FOR MOST PEOPLE, EXPERIENCE IS the best teacher—
for obvious reasons. But not for my son Jordan. He has to learn
many lessons intellectually rather than through experiencing
them. He is one of the few people worldwide who live with
congenital insensitivity to pain. In short, he doesn't feel pain
the way that you and I do. Accordingly, we've made many
trips to the emergency room because for Jordan, diving on
the driveway is the same as diving on the grass. He has never
learned to avoid sharp or abrasive objects because the resulting
cuts and stitches are not unpleasant sensations to him.

We've had doctor visits turn into hospital stays because of
small cuts he had on his foot. If you or I had a sore foot, we'd
naturally stay off it until the pain subsided. Not Jordan. As he

runs around without sensing the pain, it's easy for a small cut to become infected. The infection then spreads into the bone, and he has to stay in the hospital until it heals.

As a result, we're still trying to explain to our young son— in a way that he can grasp intellectually—that certain things can be a problem and need to be avoided. He still doesn't know that these things are hurting him. He only knows that some things will cause him to stay in the hospital while we go home.

If only he could use the experience of pain to learn. "We cannot learn without pain," noted Aristotle, and without the negative feedback of pain that God allows in our lives, we would miss many of life's most important lessons.

Many of these lessons we'd rather not learn at all. I'd rather be able to pass on to my children the things that I've learned the hard way, allowing them to skip over those painful experiences altogether. But I know that, just like with Jordan, some lessons won't register without the actual pain.

Or on the flip side, in discussing his scientific accomplishments, Isaac Newton wrote, "If I have seen further it is by standing upon the shoulders of giants."

Whether those giants are parents teaching their children or friends and family who have proven that their counsel can be trusted, Newton was referring to those people who look out for our best interests and help us become all we were intended to be. True giants have proven that they are wise, experienced, and loyal—strong enough to hold us on their shoulders.

At its essence, that is what mentoring is: building character into the lives of others and leaving a legacy.

Helping a Bunch

Of all the great people I've had the privilege of coaching over the years, Derrick Brooks is one of my favorites. Not only is he a great player and incredibly bright—Derrick graduated early from Florida State and finished high school with a 3.94 GPA—but he has also always been concerned with giving back.

After he arrived in Tampa in 1995, Derrick started hanging out at a local Boys & Girls Club. He wanted to give back, since he had received so much from his Boys Club when he was growing up in Pensacola. Derrick initially anticipated starting a ticket program to give kids a chance to attend our games, but he ended up wanting to do more than that. He was looking to really build into their lives.

His idea was to take the kids on an educational trip, something he hoped would be not only fun but also inspiring. Derrick developed a yearlong curriculum in which the kids chose a place they would like to visit and then spent a year learning about their destination. The first year, those completing the program accompanied Derrick to Atlanta to visit The King Center, the official living memorial dedicated to the advancement of Dr. Martin Luther King Jr.'s legacy. Before the trip, the kids learned everything they could about Dr. King, the leader of America's greatest nonviolent movement for justice, equality, and peace.

Derrick was amazed by the number of kids who had never been outside of Tampa, and he committed himself to broadening their horizons and motivating them to think of themselves as future leaders who could make a difference in their world.

In 2000, Derrick asked Lauren and me to travel with that year's group. *Sounds great*, I thought. They'd been to Atlanta and to Washington, D.C., but I knew Derrick was thinking about somewhere farther.

"We'd be honored to help," I told him. "Where to?"

"Africa," Derrick said with that infectious smile of his. And so we accompanied his group to South Africa and Swaziland. We traveled for ten days, went on a safari, and visited Nelson Mandela's jail cell, all the while broadening our own horizons as we broadened the children's. Derrick is building into the lives of others. The work he is doing is adding value to a life—to many lives.

That is mentoring. That is leaving a legacy. And thankfully for the kids at the Boys & Girls Clubs, that is Derrick Brooks. Last year, the first wave of the "Brooks Bunch" graduated from college, and there's no doubt in my mind that Derrick's involvement, his going the extra mile for them, played a big part in many of those kids' successes.

Like Derrick, Warrick Dunn has also looked outside himself to help others ever since he came to the NFL. Warrick came to Tampa Bay two years after Derrick as one of our first-round picks in the 1997 draft, and his desire was to help single mothers purchase homes. Since that time, he has helped with the down payments for scores of homes and has mobilized companies and other organizations to help furnish those homes.

Derrick and Warrick are special individuals, but both will tell you that they aren't doing anything extraordinary. They are merely reaching back to help someone get to a better place, giving a hand up to provide opportunities that could assist others, to use the gifts that God has given them and look beyond themselves to make a difference.

Not everyone has the financial means to take students on trips or make down payments on houses. But I don't believe that's really the most important part of what these guys have done. The mentoring they do takes more than just their financial resources. It takes their time. It requires the sacrifice of other things they could be doing for themselves.

Teachers do this every day. There are plenty of other vocations that teachers could pursue, jobs that would pay them more money and cause them less stress. But they choose to give up material things in order to build into the lives of young people. They choose to mentor. To leave a legacy.

Look outside of yourself for someone you can reach out to. You don't have to be an NFL head coach to do it. My most satisfying interactions have been with young men who didn't know what I did for a living. They only knew that I was willing to stop, listen, care, and help.

It's true for you, too. Our young men need mentors, and you can be one, with whatever gifts and experiences you bring. Trust me; there is a child out there who needs to know that you care.

KEYS TO LIFTING YOUR FRIENDS AND OTHERS

1. Choose friends for the sake of friendship, based on values.
2. Listen to the voices of those you trust, not the voices of the crowd.
3. Be open to taking advice from people whose judgment you trust.
4. Conflict can be positive. Don't fear it.

5. When conflict occurs, attack the issue, not the person.

6. Be yourself. Others may need your example, whether you realize it or not.

7. Be intentional about helping others. Give back as you move through life.

PART IV

YOUR FULL POTENTIAL

✦ ✦ ✦

Don't think you're on the right road
just because it's a well-beaten path.

AUTHOR UNKNOWN

CHAPTER 12

POWERFUL THOUGHTS

What I always feared has happened to me.
What I dreaded has come true.
   JOB 3:25

LIFE IS CHALLENGING. I wish I could tell you that you'll always be on top of the mountain, but the reality is that there are days when nothing will go right, when not only will you not be on top, you may not even be able to figure out which way is up. Do yourself a favor, and don't make it any harder than it has to be. In those moments,

> be careful how you speak to yourself;
> be careful how you think of yourself;
> be careful how you conduct yourself;
> be careful how you develop yourself.

Be Positive

We have an amazing ability to accomplish whatever our minds tell us we can do, a phenomenon that has been recognized throughout history. The great American novelist Henry James directed, "Be not afraid of life. Believe that life is worth living, and your belief will help create the fact." James could have been a football coach. The first thing you have to do when you're trying to turn a football franchise from a loser to a winner is create the *belief* that you can win. Most of the time the talent is already there to accomplish great things, but there is no belief that it will happen.

Our minds are powerful instruments and should not be taken lightly. I don't exactly know how it works, but I have heard about prisoners of war who returned home after being released and were able to play golf or perform other skills they didn't have prior to their solitary confinement. While they had been held captive, they had merely visualized what they wanted to accomplish. Obviously, the idea of mind over matter has some merit.

All football teams rely on visualization to increase their chances of success. Players visualize in different ways. Some have the ability to just see a diagram in the playbook and visualize themselves in that situation. Others have to see the play on videotape, while still others have to actually do it on the field. That's what we work on in practice. We run the plays that we will use in the game and fine-tune them against our "look squad." The look squad consists of our backup players, whose function is to simulate the other team's techniques as closely as possible so our first-team players see exactly how our plays will work during a game. By running a play several times during the week, and seeing it successfully executed, we can visualize exactly how it's going to look on Sunday. If we've been sharp in practice, then we have confidence that it will go the same way during the game.

All players work on visualization, but probably nowhere is it more important than with kickers. Adam Vinatieri has been one of the premier kickers in the NFL for the last ten years and is generally regarded as the best pressure kicker in the league. His success depends on his ability to block out all other thoughts and stimuli and just visualize his foot hitting the ball properly and the ball going through the uprights. He has developed a pre-kick routine and attempts to do everything the same, thinking about the same things on every kick, whether it's a practice kick during the week or a Super Bowl game winner. And that's why Adam is so good—that laser focus. When kickers get in trouble, it's because they allow themselves to think about other things: the distance, the wind conditions, the other team's rushers, or the stakes. That's why you'll see opposing coaches call time-out before a big kick. They're trying to "ice" the kicker, hoping to get him out of his routine and give him a chance to get distracted. But great kickers like Adam don't allow their minds to stray. They simply continue with their routine and stay focused on that small spot where their foot will connect with the ball, visualizing the end result.

Adam also has the ability to forget about past failures and stay positive. Every kicker is going to miss a field goal somewhere along the way, but Adam never lets those misses affect his next kick. He analyzes what went wrong—after all, now he's got another experience to learn from—but when it's time for the next kick, he trusts his ability and his practice regimen and he gets back into his routine, believing that the next kick is going to be perfect. And it usually is.

Being disciplined in your approach to each day of your life and accomplishing the things you dream of starts by disciplining your thoughts. Focus on those things that you *want* to occur, not those that you do *not want* to occur. In 1951, Brooklyn Dodgers pitcher Ralph Branca delivered the fateful pitch that Bobby Thomson hit for a home run for the New York Giants that has become known as the "Shot Heard 'round the World" (with obvious apologies to the minutemen at Lexington and Concord). Legend has it that the final words a teammate said to Branca just before throwing the pitch were along the lines of, "Whatever you do, don't throw it up and in."

I'll leave it to you to guess the location of the pitch.

I'm not suggesting that life will be easy or blessings will be showered upon you if you simply start thinking positively; but what I am suggesting is that negative thinking can't help but set you back. Bill Russell, an NBA all-star for years with the Boston Celtics and one of the all-time greatest winners in any sport, understood the importance of positive as well as negative thinking. "The idea is not to block every shot. The idea is to make your opponent believe that you might block every shot," he said. If the opponent was afraid of having his shot blocked—thinking negatively—Russell knew he didn't have to always try to block it. Instead of focusing on putting the ball into the basket, the opponent would adjust his shot and his approach to the basket, shift his eye contact from his goal to Russell, and eventually miss shots because he was certain that Russell could be everywhere at once on the court.

He couldn't, of course, but a little bit of doubt can do a lot of damage, especially if it becomes the focus of your thoughts.

Whatever we tend to think will often be the outcome of any given situation. I'm inclined to think there is an actual law of "self-fulfilling prophecies," and if there isn't, there probably should be. I have watched too many teams that have taken the field feeling as if it wasn't their day, only to find out at the end of the game that it indeed wasn't. I have also been a part of many more teams that have headed out of the locker room—at the beginning of the game or after half-time adjustments—expecting to make every tackle and block, execute every play, and come out victorious at the end of the game. And they did. Sure, preparation and talent go a long way toward creating that positive belief—but more often than not, it's the expectation of success that defines championship teams.

Building expectations is something we all have to do. It's hard to graduate from college when no one else in your family has done it and no one seems to expect you to do it either. How can you develop those positive thoughts and nurture the belief that you *can* do it?

When I started coaching in the NFL in 1981, there were fourteen African American assistant coaches in the whole league, and no head coaches or coordinators. I didn't show up my first day of work thinking that I was going to be a head coach and win a Super Bowl, but I *did* think about the future. I wanted to learn as much as I could and do my job well. I believed that if I did that, I'd get promoted within the organization. And I didn't let the fact that there were no black men in those high-level jobs put a damper on my thinking. I always believed that, because of who I was working for and the people around me, I would learn enough to be an excellent coach. If I became good enough, then it would just be a matter of getting the opportunity.

That part I couldn't control, so I had to leave the opportunities in God's hands. But I never once allowed myself to believe that I couldn't do the job if I got the chance. And over the next fifteen years, even when I wasn't sure I would ever get that chance, I had to keep negativity out of my thought process and leave it with God.

You won't always rise to the level of the expectations you have for yourself, but you will never be able to rise above the imaginary ceiling you construct in your mind. How high do you want to set those expectations? How high would you like to go?

Your life will also be affected by how much you allow the things around you—like a shot blocker—to affect the direction of your journey. You will not be able to do anything about removing all the distractions you find along the way. The key is to continue to focus your thoughts on where you want to go, regardless of those distractions. What do you want your tomorrow to look like? Allow your mind and heart to embrace that direction.

Salt Water or Fresh

Writing about the power of the tongue, New Testament author James notes that both fresh and salt water cannot flow from the same spring,[10] or as my friend Ken Whitten says, "What's down in the well will come up in the bucket."

What is down in your well? From what source does the water in your well come? From where do you draw strength and direction for your life?

---

[10] See James 3:11–12.

The writer of Hebrews recounted incident after incident of saints who had demonstrated that the source of their strength came from God, even without being able to see the end of the journey He had set out for them. They imagined and believed in a future painted by the hand of the One who had proven His faithfulness to them time and time again. Their lives and hearts—and their visions for their futures—were shaped by their faith in God and by the vision He had set before them.

The apostle Paul, in his letter to the church in Philippi, offered some good advice to live by in Philippians 4:8-9:

Finally, brothers, whatever is true, whatever is noble, whatever is right, whatever is pure, whatever is lovely, whatever is admirable—if anything is excellent or praiseworthy—think about such things. Whatever you have learned or received or heard from me, or seen in me—put it into practice. And the God of peace will be with you. (NIV)

What's down in your well? Whatever is there will govern the thoughts for your today and your tomorrow.

Fill it well.

CHAPTER 13

EDUCATION AND ATHLETICS

*"Son, looks to me like you're spending too much time
on one subject."*

SHELBY METCALF, TEXAS A&M BASKETBALL COACH,
TO A PLAYER WHO RECEIVED ONE D AND FOUR Fs

IF THERE WERE EVER AREAS in which we seem to
have switched the price tags, it's in the areas of education and
athletics. If we could choose the future for our young sons,
how many of us would choose that they get a Ph.D. in physics
over becoming the starting shortstop for the New York Yankees? For most of us, I think the answer would probably be,
"Tony, I simply want what's best for him and wouldn't want
to force him to play for the Yankees. A small-market team
would be fine, too." You can probably write a similar conversation for the futures we have in mind for our daughters.

I must admit, I feel that pull as well. It's hard not to—our
society places great weight on athletic achievement. (The irony

that you're reading this book, written by a sports figure, is not lost on me.) Yet in your most rational moments, in thinking through the full implications of, for instance, life in the NFL—a profession with an average career of 3.3 years, in which the possibility of permanent physical injury is always present, that offers limited and underdeveloped skills off the athletic field, and is marked by broken marriages and dysfunctional families—would you really choose that over a future that could make your child happy and able to contribute to society? We shouldn't, but sadly, many of us do.

We see it again and again. We see it when children are encouraged or, worse, pushed to compete in sports. We see it in the overzealous Little League parents who have lost all touch with reality when it comes to their children. We see it when parents, and sometimes coaches, try to live vicariously through their children's athletic achievements, which they always dreamed of for themselves. The cold, hard facts are that far less than one percent—more like one-tenth of one percent—of high school athletes will grow up to be professional athletes. Over the last ten years, the average rookie crop in the NFL has contained five Indiana natives per year. That means of all the high school seniors in Indiana this year who dream of playing professional football, five of them will make it—and that might be for just one year. You can only imagine how small that percentage might be for Little Leaguers.

In the meantime, those children are often not encouraged to spend the same time and attention obtaining a full and complete education, even though the odds are that high school athletes will need to use that education in their lives more than their athletic training. Even for the players who do make it to the NFL and are making more money than most people their age, those post-career skills are crucial. Given that average career of 3.3 years, most guys will be around twenty-six years old when that big money stops coming in, and they'll still have most of their adult lives ahead of them. As they start to look for work, they begin to understand that in this new job market, athletic skills don't count for much. And all too often, their nonathletic skills have never been nurtured.

The other side effect of this focus on athletic achievement is that the true meaning has often been lost, submerged in a society that idolizes sports. Sports should be about enjoyment, cooperation, team building, learning to deal with adversity, building character, and pursuing excellence. But those days are going the way of eight-track tapes and twelve-inch televisions. Growing up, I played a lot of sports because I liked to. They were fun, and I enjoyed the challenge of learning how to do new things like hit a two-iron or ice-skate backward. Ironically, football was one of the last sports I learned how to play on an organized level.

Unfortunately, most kids today don't get to have fun like that with their youth sports. I hear all too many stories of eight-year-olds who have given up other sports because one coach thinks they should pursue a single sport year-round, including traveling teams. Year-round? Traveling to play? At eight years old? On the off chance that your child might be that one in a million to play major league soccer or baseball or be in the Olympics? And what makes me even sadder is the fact that many of these kids aren't having fun. They're being coached and pushed like adults, with the idea that they have to be the best player on their team so they can go to "the next level."

I'm grateful that my parents supported my siblings and me in our involvement in sports and other activities, but they also wanted us to be well-rounded. As for me, somehow I was one of the one-tenth of one percent—I did have the opportunity to play professional sports, although after three years in the NFL (I fell 0.3 years short of average), I still needed other life skills to support myself as a twenty-five-year-old whose athletic career was over. However, if either my parents or coaches had wanted me to focus on one sport exclusively, I'm sure I would have chosen basketball in high school, and thereby closed off my actual playing career, as well as my coaching career. We need to give children a chance to explore and develop. Life is an adventure, and they need to be stretched beyond those activities at which they excel.

Use Athletics to Complement Your Education

Hunter Smith, our trainer with the Colts, has twin sons who just graduated from Florida State. Hunter recently returned from Tallahassee and asked if I knew the commencement speaker, Ernest Cook. I said that I did. I had gotten to know Ernie more than thirty years ago but had lost track of him over the years.

I met Ernie when I was a high school senior, during my recruiting trip to the University of Minnesota. He was in his first year of medical school there when I arrived, having finished his playing days the year before. He was drafted by an NFL club but didn't sign, choosing instead to attend medical school.

The coaches and administrators at every school that I visited gave a standard spiel to high school recruits about the education they were offering, but I found that talking to Ernie was completely different from what I had heard from everybody else. Since I had grown up with educators for parents, his message that weekend resonated with me, so much so that I still remember much of it today—thirty-five years later.

"They told me that I could go to the NFL, but I never cared about that," he told me. "Football was just a chance to get a scholarship, and the coaches here told me that they'd help me get into medical school, which they did." He had initially signed to become the first black athlete on a football scholarship at Florida State, but he received so many death threats after signing that he decided to go to Minnesota instead. I asked him why he chose not to try professional football, even though he had been drafted. I didn't know anyone at the time who wouldn't try to play if they had the chance. You could always go to medical school after you finished playing. Ernie told me, however, that his goal had never been to play pro football. It had always been to become a doctor and go back to his hometown of Daytona Beach. I was impressed and somewhat shocked by that—a talented athlete, in fact one of the university's star players, who wasn't all hyped up to play pro football and wasn't looking for the money, fame, and notoriety that went along with the NFL. Ernest wanted an uncommon route through the adventure of life. He wanted to make a difference in his hometown for other people, not just for himself.

His road was the one less traveled, and I made note of it, even at the age of seventeen. Now here he was, returning as the vice president of a national healthcare company after having been in private practice for years in Daytona Beach, speaking at a graduation ceremony of the university where, thirty-five years earlier, his life had been threatened.

Minnesota had another unusual athlete at that time as well. When I joined the University of Minnesota basketball team in December of my freshman year, I met Charles Sims, who was a junior on the basketball team and, like Ernie, there for different reasons than the rest of us. While everyone else on a basketball scholarship was hoping to develop their talents for the NBA, Charles wanted to be a dentist. He knew that basketball could pay for the first four years of what would be a very expensive dental degree. He enjoyed basketball and loved competing, but he was playing to pay for school. He did everything he could do to help us win, but he never thought about the NBA and he was the only athlete I knew at Minnesota who took his books on road trips. I respected him because he knew what he wanted to do and never allowed anything to destroy his focus.

Ernie Cook and Charles Sims inspired me to do well in school because they took the right approach to being a student-athlete. They went against the peer pressure of the environment.

It all started with college. Booker T. Washington once said, "If you can't read, it's going to be hard to realize dreams." Most of us can read, but do we have the other skills necessary for fulfilling all that we were designed to be? Make sure that you do everything in your power to give yourself that chance.

Oh, that you would not live your whole life with your talents untapped.

CHAPTER 14

CAREER, WORK, AND MONEY

The mercenaries will always beat the draftees, but the volunteers will crush them both.
CHUCK NOLL

WORK IS GOOD.

My good friend Tony Evans, a pastor in Dallas, says that we were created to work. "Before Adam had Eve, he had a job," he says. Work is good. Adding value is positive.

I've seen it time and again: high school and college students trying to figure out what they are going to do—and why. Ultimately, it's not really a career question. It's a purpose question. *What am I going to do with my life?* We all need to answer the deep questions of purpose, meaning, and fulfillment in life.

But don't be paralyzed over your career choice.

Men who have been in one line of work for over three decades are becoming dinosaurs. Even within my industry,

I've had seven employers. What you're doing today probably won't be what you're going to be doing in the distant future, and possibly not even the near future.

Rather than making choices on the basis of money, however, select something *that you want to do.* It's great to love your work, and a blessing to enjoy it.

Lousy Motivation

As the head coach, Coach Noll was concerned not only for our physical well-being but also for the emotional health of the team. He loved the quote at the beginning of this chapter about the draftees, mercenaries, and volunteers because of its truth. People who are forced into something will be least effective, while those with an external motivation (money, in the case of the mercenaries) will be effective to a point. However, those with internal drive, who have signed on for the endeavor because their *hearts* are in it, will rise to the top.

Money may get you started, but it won't be enough to sustain you when the times become difficult.

Coach Noll told me repeatedly that I should "never make a job decision based on money"—first when I was a player, then when I was one of his coaches. He wasn't disparaging money or its ability to allow you to do things in life, but rather making sure that I understood its limitations.

All too often I've seen our players in this era of salary caps forced into making a tough decision. They love playing for the Colts, they fit perfectly into our offense or defense, they really like their teammates and our coaching staff, and their wives and families are comfortable in Indianapolis. On top of all that, they're having fun. Then another team offers them $2 million more than we can pay them. When those players come into my office and ask me what they should do, I have to admit, I'm not always comfortable giving them the advice Coach Noll gave me. I worry that it might sound self-serving—that I want them to stay with us and take less money because they can help us win. But the truth is, in most cases, it really is better to disregard the money. It's just hard to do. They have so many people telling them that they would be crazy *not* to leave. What about their future, their financial security? What about providing for their families?

It's easy to compare dollars to dollars, and when we have the opportunity to earn more, it's tempting to think, *This is best for my family*, or *That employer values me more*, or *That team (or company) respects me more.* The reality is, however, money isn't really a very good measure of what's best for you or your family. In fact, the more you base critical decisions on monetary evidence, the more your children will come to believe that money is the most important thing in your life. And ultimately, in theirs.

Having said that money shouldn't drive employment decisions, I also have to say this: poor money decisions can tie your hands, reduce your options, and cause you to make bad decisions out of desperation. Credit card companies spend hundreds of millions of dollars to market their cards to students and young people—and they are not spending those amounts in order to do you a favor. That's one thing I'm glad my dad taught me—buying on credit costs you a lot of money, so whenever possible, pay cash. He always made me do extra jobs for him to get the money I needed to buy something. His explanation? Waiting until I had earned the money to buy it would be much cheaper than borrowing money from him and paying him back. The interest rates he would charge probably weren't legal, but even at a young age, I could do the math and figure out his point.

Borrowing money is expensive. That's not something the credit card companies will tell you. And it's not something we as parents today are doing a good job communicating to our kids. It's lucrative for those companies to get you to spend beyond your means, buying stuff you don't need with money you don't have. Once they get their hooks in you, it is very difficult to dig your way out. And it may limit the career choices you have down the road.

Don't do it.

You may not find that career path that gets you excited right away. Keep looking, but give your current position a chance. Many entry- and intermediate-level positions are not terribly exciting, but they may be important stepping-stones along the way. The position might involve the development of skills that feel tedious or "beneath you," but all jobs are really training for subsequent ones. Sometimes employers use entry-level positions to evaluate an employee's abilities and commitment. Many positions require trust, and employers need to know they can trust you with little things that seem menial before they will trust you with more. Be careful that you aren't evaluating a position on the wrong scale.

At the same time, keep in mind that you don't have to do it forever. Too many people decide that they'll find their "it" later, whatever *it* is they were meant to do professionally, or maybe whatever *it* means in terms of getting them involved in the community. Too many people defer their lives until they arrive somewhere—they're not certain where but figure they'll recognize it when they get there—and never truly live. Make sure that's not you.

When I played professional football, the average salary was $47,000 a year, and most guys made much less than that. So a lot of players, including me, had off-season jobs. I worked for Mellon Bank, Heinz, and Dayton-Hudson department stores. I tried a lot of things, but I never really found the job I loved—until I started coaching football. I'm thankful that I love what I'm doing. I can't imagine doing something for thirty years if I didn't.

Coach Noll loved football, but it didn't define who he was; it was merely what he did. He didn't put other parts of his life on hold. At the same time, it was clear that he was in the profession that he wanted to be in, doing what he wanted to do.

Leave Your Work *at* Work

Many of us walk in the door at the end of the day carrying our frustrations with us. We know we need to learn to let it go, but that's easier said than done. When we lose a game on a last-second field goal, it's tough for me to really be excited about playing Candy Land with the kids as soon as I get home. But I have to make myself do it. It's not their fault that we lost, and I can't let my job, which already takes me away from my kids too much, negatively impact the time I do have with them. Find a symbolic way of letting go when you get home. Some people open the mailbox on their way into the house and pretend to put work issues inside until the next day. Others touch the door frame as they enter the house the way football teams touch a mural as they leave the locker room. Whether it's your family or friends—or your blood pressure—no one deserves to be saddled with whatever happened at the office. Tomorrow will have enough problems of its own. Don't start worrying about them now. Don't let the emotion of the day govern your home life and free time.

I have always tried not to let my disappointments at work spill over to our family time, even if we lose a game. This can be very difficult at times. Lauren always understands if I've had a particularly draining game, and sometimes, if we have already made post-game plans, she gives me the option of not going through with them. The kids, however, don't always have that sensitivity. That can be a good thing, because even when I am discouraged, the kids still bounce right up to me and don't ever make me feel as if I've let the whole city down.

But on one occasion, my son Eric really put my resolve to leave work at work to the test. In 2001, we were still in Tampa, and Eric's favorite college player was Santana Moss, a wide receiver at the University of Miami. We had an opportunity to draft Moss that year with the Bucs but took an offensive tackle with our first pick instead. Eric was distraught and wouldn't talk to me the rest of draft weekend.

The New York Jets selected Moss later in the first round, so I called my good friend Herm Edwards, who was the head coach of the Jets at the time. I told him about Eric's interest in Moss and how disappointed he was that we didn't pick him. Herm responded by sending Eric a Jets jersey and some pictures signed by Moss, which raised Eric's admiration for the player to an even higher level.

After that season, I was fired by the Bucs and the next year ended up coaching the Colts into the playoffs. Whom did we play in the opening round? The Jets. In New York—Herm's team drilled us, 41–0, and I was really discouraged. It was not the way I wanted to end my first season in Indianapolis.

After the game was over, totally oblivious to my disappointment, Eric ran up to me and asked, "Dad, can you take me to the Jets' locker room so I can meet Santana?" As you might imagine, walking into the Jets' locker room was the last thing I wanted to do at that moment. Fortunately, I remembered my pledge not to let my job disappointments affect my time with the kids, so I took Eric over to visit with Moss. It was extremely difficult going in there and seeing the Jets celebrating, but I knew it was important to Eric, and it's something he still remembers to this day.

Maybe you, like me, are in a position of direct leadership. I try to remain cognizant of the fact that I have eighteen coaches who work with me and another group of staff members in various capacities. Each of them has a family that he will go home to when he leaves work. If I put unnecessary stress on my group, my behavior can have a widespread, unintended effect. Although I strive to model Christ's example anyway, keeping this in mind provides another reason for me not to be a jerk.

But Go Home

Some people use work as an escape from their home lives, simply ignoring anything that doesn't have to do with their careers. I see that all the time in my profession. As sportswriter Frank Deford has noted, football coaches are some of the only professionals who congratulate themselves on how long they work. Anywhere else, you would be fired if the only way you could do your job was to sleep at the office—night after night, week after week.

His tongue-in-cheek analysis (I hope it was tongue-in-cheek, anyway) is absolutely correct. Denny Green, our head coach when I was the defensive coordinator of the Minnesota Vikings, taught me that it takes three days to prepare for a game. Even on weeks when we have an extra day or two because of the schedule, we take three solid, long days to prepare for a game, same as always. That's it. But too often I see other coaches spend every available hour and every extra day watching one more tape or diagramming one more play.

Your job is like that too, I suspect. There's always something you could be doing. Always more preparation, more research, more to do to get ahead. But at some point I think we have to be willing to stand behind what we've done. When you've given a solid day's work, that should be enough.

And when you get home, be home. Your mind will no doubt wander to your work—if you've allowed it to leave your work at all—but try to keep that to a minimum. Your friends, your wife, your children—and even you yourself—deserve quality, fully committed time. And if you haven't already experienced it yourself, take my word for it: children know when you're there simply as a warm body but otherwise a thousand miles away. You have to make a conscious effort not to do that. Go home and disengage from the trials and troubles of the office.

Coach Noll really enjoyed spending time with his family, cooking, flying planes, and listening to jazz. For me, it's my family, church and community activities, and fishing. Make sure that you're not so busy making a living that you forget to actually *live*.

Live! Now!

CHAPTER 15

GOALS AND RISK

Security is mostly a superstition. It does not exist in nature, nor do the children of men as a whole experience it. Avoiding danger is no safer in the long run than outright exposure. Life is either a daring adventure or nothing.

HELEN KELLER

MATT EMMONS IS A WORLD-CHAMPION marksman. In the 2004 Summer Olympics in Athens, Greece, he had a significant lead when he entered the final round of the 50-meter, three-position rifle competition. He hit the bull's-eye on his three shots, then looked on, puzzled, as the automatic scoring system did not credit his shots. He called the judge over, and the target was pulled in to ascertain just what had occurred. It was untouched. No holes.

The target in the next lane, however, had three extra holes—holes made by Matt's shots. His mistake cost him in the standings, and he finished eighth. This story illustrates my point that without a goal—your *own* goal, not someone else's—you won't reach all that you're capable of. Unless you are focused on the passions of your heart and are striving toward them, you won't achieve all that God has in store for you.

Of course, life isn't neat and tidy, and the story doesn't end there. Competitor Katerina Kurkova of the Czech Republic made it a point to introduce herself and offer her condolences to Matt, the American shooter who had just made such a huge blunder. Less than three years later, they were married. You never know what God has in store for you, even from your disappointments.[11]

My goals are usually qualitative rather than quantitative. I never aim for a particular number of games to win, but rather for a team that is as good as it can be and guys who are an asset to the community and good role models. Those are the things I reflect on at the end of each year as I analyze our season. I measure our teams by how we performed compared to our potential—that's really the only reasonable measurement to use.

As for me personally, I try to improve each year. When I was a young assistant, my goal was to learn enough to be a good defensive coach and to help my players play as well as possible. Later, it was to continue to learn and improve, so that I might merit consideration as a defensive coordinator. Still later, it was to put myself in a position to someday become a head coach.

---

[11] Matt Emmons was in position for a gold medal in the same event in Beijing, China, in 2008 when his trigger went off before he anticipated, costing him the gold. He conducted himself with the same dignity that he had in 2004, prompting the head of the International Olympic Committee, Jacques Rogge, to publicly commend the quality of his character. Now *that* is a legacy.

Take note, however. Though I wanted to be a coordinator and head coach, I continued to focus on a goal that was within my control: to continually hone my coaching abilities in order to be ready for those positions. I couldn't control whether or not I was hired. Some things are up to others—and God—and therefore aren't realistic to hold over yourself.

Sometimes, those goals require risk. The old saying that "you can't steal second with your foot still on first" is true not only in baseball but also in life. When Herm Edwards left my staff in Tampa Bay to become the head coach of the New York Jets, I was forced to replace a terrific coach. Fortunately, given our success and the fact that it was one of only thirty-two NFL positions, the applicants were many.

I hired Mike Tomlin, a young—very young—coach out of the University of Cincinnati. Mike had been at the university for only two years, but I hired him because I loved what I saw: a teacher with a high energy level. Some people may have thought of this as taking a chance because I was replacing a highly respected veteran NFL coach with someone who had no NFL experience.

Mike was the one who took a bigger risk, however. He had been safe in Cincinnati, secure in his current coaching position. Yet he decided to step out of his comfort zone to join a staff that was undergoing transition, a club in which rumors were circulating as to whether any of us would keep our jobs if we didn't go to the Super Bowl. By coming with us, Mike could have very easily been out of a job the following season. Though many would think that coming to the Buccaneers from the University of Cincinnati was a no-brainer, Mike had to consider his options and take a chance.

That risk paid off. I did get fired after that season, but

Mike stayed on with Tampa for four more seasons; then he joined Minnesota for one year as their defensive coordinator. Seven years after his decision not to play it safe, Mike was named the head coach of the Pittsburgh Steelers.

Sometimes, taking a risk doesn't necessarily pay off. When it was time for me to leave the Steelers in 1988, Lauren and I really agonized over our options. I was offered jobs by two coaches who ended up in the Hall of Fame, both in the same off-season: Bill Parcells of the Giants and Bill Walsh of the 49ers. I also had good interviews with Sam Wyche in Cincinnati and Marty Schottenheimer in Kansas City. All four men were great coaches and good people. I had played for Bill Walsh and Sam Wyche when I was in San Francisco, and I knew I could be comfortable with either. Of course, Bill Parcells had recently won his first Super Bowl, and my interview with him was a defensive coach's dream: sitting in an office, talking football theory with Bill and his staff—Bill Belichick and Romeo Crennel.

However, Lauren and I were in the process of starting a family, and we decided that the cities of New York and San Francisco were more than we wanted to undertake. I didn't get offered the job in Cincinnati, so we ended up with Marty Schottenheimer in Kansas City.

The quality of life in Kansas City was great, and it was a perfect place to start raising children. But after three years with the Chiefs, I felt I needed to move on, for reasons that were more personal than professional. In the meantime, the Giants and 49ers had each won a Super Bowl. It would have been easy to second-guess my decision, but there really is no safe path through life. We make decisions with the best information we have, which often makes it seem like we're in a fog. (This can feel especially true during games.)

What I've learned is to gather as much information as possible at the time, pray about things, make a decision, and move on. Certainly, I learn from my decisions and the consequences so I don't repeat mistakes in the future, but I don't second-guess choices I've already made. It isn't productive. Even though we didn't win a Super Bowl in Kansas City, many of the things I learned and many of the relationships I made there are still benefiting me today.

Unless you get a second chance to undo those decisions, it's best to press on and give yourself a break, while doing the best you can with where you are. Some of your decisions will pan out; some will be disasters. One great life lesson I've learned from sports is that no one wins every game. And we *can* win championships even after losing some games. Either way, we've won in my book, because we stepped out of the illusion of safety and security and are fully active in the game of life.

Sometimes others will second-guess your decisions, especially if they don't share your view of the world. Many people believe that you should never pass up advancement at work—and the resulting money or status. If you are a father who passes up a promotion—or quits a position—because you are not involved enough at home, or because you are in a location that isn't conducive to raising children, the critics will suggest that you're being irresponsible.

Don't listen to them. Have the courage of your convictions.

Be uncommon.

CHAPTER 16

ALCOHOL AND DRUGS

Drunkenness is simply voluntary insanity.
    SENECA

THE NFL DRAFT IS a two-day event that is the culmination of a year's worth of scouting. The scouts are on the road for months at a time, and the personnel directors and general managers of the various franchises also travel extensively— and when they're not traveling, they are watching tape. Even the coaches get into the act for many clubs, either watching tape or attending workouts, or both, during the final month or so before the draft.

By the time the draft arrives, everyone is understandably on edge but ready to go. The process is wearying: the mock drafts, philosophical debates of need versus overall talent, hot lists of players who might be available, discussions of character, analysis of the trade market, and the simple logistics of setting up the draft boards.

And all that takes place before the two days of the draft begin. The clubs send representatives to New York for the event, while the rest of us stay behind at club headquarters, eating, talking, watching film—just once more!—and manning the phones. At the end of day two, when it's all over, the entire organization is exhausted.

In April 2001, a group of us were gathered in Jerry Angelo's office at our team headquarters, having just completed what would turn out to be my final draft with the Buccaneers. It was around ten o'clock at night, and we were chatting about the completed draft and other topics. The offices were snug, and the six of us were seated on extra chairs or any available surface. Shortly thereafter, I headed home.

My coauthor, Nathan, who was part of the Bucs' scouting department at the time, was also in the room, and as soon as the door closed behind me, he was ordered to his feet. "Get up!" He looked around, confused, and the command was given again.

As he stood, he realized the towel he had been sitting on was covering the beer cooler. Out of respect for me, they had waited until I was gone.

I had tried to tell those guys for years that even though I don't drink, I didn't mind if they did. I don't mind parties—Jesus went to plenty of parties. And just because drinking isn't the right choice for me, it doesn't mean that others can't partake; after all, Jesus' first miracle was turning water into wine. Even so, for whatever reason, they wouldn't drink around me.

As I said, I don't have a problem with anyone having a drink. What I do mind is our society's inability to see alcohol for what it truly is: a drug. We have, rightly I think, strongly warned our children about tobacco and illegal drugs, but I am concerned about what sometimes seems to be a "look the other way" relationship with alcohol. And the example this sets for our young people is particularly disturbing. We don't allow anyone to drink who is under the age of twenty-one, which I completely agree with. The unintended consequence of that law, however, is unfortunate. Because they can't legally drink until twenty-one, many young men now view that twenty-first birthday drink as a rite of passage into manhood. The law seems to have made drinking more attractive because it is forbidden until then.

I'm very sensitive to this issue, based upon my profession and its financial relationships with alcohol. Our league derives a great deal of revenue from alcohol sponsorships, which certainly helps to pay my salary. It's the one aspect of working in the NFL that I really struggle with when I'm asked about it. (On the other hand, I have no problem, for instance, when people ask how I, as a Christian, can be involved in playing such a violent game on Sundays. That's an easy one for me.) I know that my work indirectly promotes alcohol consumption on dangerous levels. Personally, I would be willing to live with less money if it would help keep even one kid from making a mistake. I think we'd all be better for it.

A Father's Decision

As I have reflected on my father's influence in my life, one of the things I am most grateful for is that he chose not to drink any alcohol. It would have been fine if he did, but his abstinence was a powerful example for me, maybe even more than he might have realized at the time. Whether in high school or college, whenever I found myself in a situation in which everybody was drinking, I always thought of my dad. Because someone that I respected so highly had chosen to not drink, I could make the same choice with confidence.

"No thanks, guys."

In addition to my dad, I also benefited from positive peer pressure. On the flight home after my first road game as a member of the Steelers, I saw that the flight attendants were passing out beer. I didn't drink, but as the new guy on the team, I was still a little nervous, not sure what to do.

Then I noticed some of the guys were giving the beers back or giving them away, so I did the same. It was a moment of positive peer pressure for me and brought home the truth of Romans 14:21: "It is better not to eat meat or drink wine or do anything else if it might cause another believer to stumble." Their example on that plane ride home helped me not to stumble.

As for any other mind-altering substances, my advice is simple: just don't bother. The upside is so limited and fleeting—a chance for escape, I suppose—but the downside, coming either from one bad decision or a lifetime of addiction struggles, is not worth it.

We had a player with the Colts who had worked his way from being an undrafted player out of college to being a starter for our team. All that changed when he was stopped for a speeding violation. The officer noticed a smell of marijuana in the car and found some in the vehicle. The player was arrested, and by the end of the next day, he was no longer a Colt. This player knew our organization's stance on drugs. The whole course of his professional career changed in one moment. But that's nothing compared to Len Bias. After being an NBA first-round pick in 1986, Bias's life ended at twenty-two as the result of a cocaine overdose. Eight days after Bias's death, twenty-three-year-old Don Rogers, a Pro Bowl free safety for the Cleveland Browns, died the same way at his bachelor party the night before he was to be married.

Every day, young people die as a result of alcohol and drug abuse. They're usually not as high profile as these two young men, but their deaths are just as tragic. Because I've never used drugs, I don't know how good they can temporarily make you feel. But no matter how good it is, I simply can't believe it could be worth the risk.

I know there are many people who can "drink responsibly," as the commercials urge us to do. But can you really be sure? How do you know that you'll be able to remain in control? How do you know you won't have one too many? Are you sure you won't become addicted?

I heard Tony Campolo, a professor at Eastern University in Pennsylvania, tell a story of attending an on-campus party one year. He headed into the bathroom and saw a student on his knees, clutching the toilet. Through bleary eyes, the kid stared up at him and spoke.

"Great party, huh?"

Be careful with alcohol, and don't get near anything else that's mind-altering. It's just not worth being part of the crowd in that way, and the downside may be far worse than the upside could ever be.

CHAPTER 17

FAILURE

Only those who dare to fail greatly can ever achieve greatly.
ROBERT F. KENNEDY

I REALLY WISH I HAD learned more about failure when I was young.

I didn't realize just how often it would rear its ugly head. I saw successful people—either in their jobs, in sports, or with their families—and didn't have much of an appreciation for the hard work and the setbacks that go along with that success. I'm often introduced today as one of only three people to win a Super Bowl as a player and as a head coach. What they don't always say is that there were twenty-seven straight seasons that ended in disappointment between those two Super Bowl wins.

The beauty of what I've learned through a life in sports, however, is that failure happens—regularly. And failure, as it turns out, is a constant in the human experience. I've also learned that if you're afraid of failure, you won't try to do very much. But if you're going to chase meaningful dreams and do significant things, you have to be willing to come up short sometimes. I hope that you will fail less than I have, but even so, we all fail. Count on it. The more I learned about those people I admired for their successes, the more I also began to admire them for the way they handled failures. Success is really a journey of persistence and perseverance in spite of failure.

In some ways, failure feels like a dirty little secret because people rarely want to discuss their own failures. But in reality, we're all wearing masks to cover our shortcomings, all thinking that the feelings of self-doubt and misgiving are ours alone. Nothing could be further from the truth; failure is part of being human.

The topic of failure belongs in the general category of facing adversity. The difference, I suppose, is that failure is viewed as a result, while adversity is seen as something you work your way through. To truly accomplish your goals, however, I think failure has to be viewed as part of the process. Thomas Edison said that he didn't fail repeatedly; he merely found ten thousand ways *not* to make a lightbulb.

The journey through adversity is inevitable if we're striving for improvement. If things are progressing smoothly, where's the need for self-examination and growth? Why would we stop and evaluate how we could have done something better if we were always successful, always reaching the outcomes we have set our sights on? Our players lift weights constantly and have refined their bodies in the process. They have learned through the adversity and failure of being beaten by someone stronger on the other side of the line that they need to improve to succeed. My dad, the physiologist, explained to me that in weight lifting, the muscle fibers are broken down when they are stressed, which then leads to muscle growth. The same is true for other kinds of growth.

Through pressure, stress, and adversity, we are strengthened—in our character, in our faith, and in our ability to get out of bed again and give it one more try.

Toughness

I was recently talking about hardships with James Brown, the studio host of *The NFL on CBS*. He said that he has been called an "overnight success," and then he shook his head and laughed. "Yeah. After the first twenty years of toiling, sure . . . then it was overnight."

To me, this shows toughness. Our players so often talk about being "tough," but I'm not sure they grasp what that truly means. Toughness is shown in how you respond to adversity. Can you respond without losing your footing and your direction? If so, that shows me that you're tough. Life is messy. We don't always get a happy ending, and sometimes the middle isn't so happy either. You never really know how tough people are until they encounter the rough spots. We're all tough when things are going our way. We're all tough when we're getting the breaks. That's easy.

But the truly tough man is the one who stays grounded in his values and focused on his goals when things are challenging. When things in life don't go according to plan, the tough man will exhibit a determination to reach his goal no matter the obstacles.

I try to give our players some latitude and allow them to

fail so they can learn to respond to problems and then grow. Toughness, even on the football field, is more appropriately thought of as mental, not physical, endurance.

People often ask the question, "Why does God allow bad things to happen to good people?" Obviously, there are no easy answers to that question. But I do know this: God is constantly working in us through it all, molding and shaping us into what He created us to be, and it's in the valleys of our failures where He is working the hardest, making us into something uncommon.

KEYS FOR YOUR FULL POTENTIAL

1. Be positive. Your mind is more powerful than you think.
2. Build high expectations into others.
3. What is down in the well comes up in the bucket. Fill yourself with positive things.
4. Your education matters. Don't cut corners—you'll only cheat yourself if you don't learn the material.
5. Sports are great . . . as a *complement* to academics.
6. Find employment that excites you for reasons beyond the salary.
7. Make conservative decisions with debt.
8. Don't take hassles from work home with you.
9. Goals are important, but make sure they are worthy goals—you just might reach them!
10. Don't fear risk—life is an adventure, not a dress rehearsal.
11. Make the best decisions you can after deliberation and prayer, but don't second-guess yourself. You did the best you could.
12. Be careful with mind-altering substances, even legal ones. Addiction can sneak up and destroy your life.

13. Don't be afraid to be different.

14. You will fail. Remember that, but don't fear it.

15. True toughness is how you respond to adversity.

PART V

ESTABLISH A MISSION THAT MATTERS

+ + +

The opposite
of courage in
our society is
not cowardice,
it is conformity.

ROLLO MAY

CHAPTER 18

STYLE VERSUS SUBSTANCE

Don't settle for style. Succeed in substance.
Wynton Marsalis

WHEN I WAS A BOY, my parents always made sure that I had the proper equipment for whatever activity I was involved in at a given time—usually sports. That meant shoes and practice gear that fit and were functional—functional being the key word.

I have a vivid recollection of eighth grade—1968—and wanting a pair of Chuck Taylor basketball shoes. Everybody had a pair, and I mean everybody. They were Converse's most popular shoe—the Converse All-Star, a canvas high-top. It's hard to imagine today, but back then . . . wow.

My father took me to the store for new shoes. I wanted the Chuck Taylors, which were $7.99, as I recall. My dad thought that I should get the Kmart version, which retailed for $3.99. I was distressed.

My dad showed me that Kmart's store brand and the Converse shoes were made of the same material, with the same quality, and that the price difference of a 100-percent markup was due to all the marketing hype. I tried to explain how important it was to have the cool shoes and how I didn't want to stand out from everyone else by wearing the Kmart shoes. It wasn't the marketing that I was concerned about, I told him. It was the opinions of all my friends. I had seen the advertisements that promised these shoes would make me part of the group.

My dad didn't say that I couldn't get the shoes; he just said that *he* wouldn't spend the extra money to buy them. His obligation was to provide me with safe, comfortable equipment for my activities. If I wanted to go beyond that, it was up to me. I remember what he said that day: "They are identical, but if it matters enough to you, then you can earn the four dollars to pay the difference." It was my first lesson in style versus substance.

I chose the Chuck Taylors, understanding that I was choosing style. And I worked extra jobs beyond my regular chores for a month to pay off the four dollars my dad had advanced me to buy the shoes.

Perception versus Reality

Today, I talk to our team regularly about perception versus reality. The battle between style and substance happens in football a lot, just as it does in life. Certain players are perceived by fans and the media as different people than the ones their families and friends know. Certain teams are looked at in ways that may not be accurate. Analysts are always using terms like "a finesse team, a physical team, a dome team, an offensive team," and so on.

But to win and be effective, I want our players to know

what they're really dealing with, so we try to dig beyond the perception and look at the reality. Perceptions are built by a lot of things: reputations, media portrayals, sometimes even past performance. Uncovering reality sometimes requires a little work.

The first step in developing a good game plan is to determine who we really are—or should be—beyond the perceptions of the world and beyond the lure of who society says we should be. It's important to know exactly who you are, both individually and as a team. You need to know your strengths and weaknesses, as well as those of your opponent. That's also a good first step in developing a solid game plan for becoming an uncommon man.

There are a lot of perceptions today about manhood, masculinity, and how to succeed in this world. I think we have to look deeper into things and use resources like the Bible to help us define what manhood truly is. Some of the definitions that our young men are living by today don't give them a chance to succeed.

One of the most compelling and distorted perceptions is that respect comes from status. We tend to focus on what we do, how much we earn, what we look like, what we wear, and what we have. Therefore, it becomes important to us to have a job that will provide the type of status we want, as well as enough income to be able to buy the stuff that will add to that status. It's important to dress a certain way and to go to certain schools. The media equates all these things with a certain level of respect. We see it in popular culture—played up in magazines, television shows, and movies. Such a constant onslaught perpetuates the perception that respect comes from status.

And then, all too often, we begin to view and evaluate other people that way as well. If they don't have certain types of jobs, if they don't dress a certain way, if they don't have money or the material things that we equate with a certain level of status, we decide that they probably aren't successful and don't have significance, and therefore we don't respect them.

With this mind-set, status becomes one of the most important measures of a man's masculinity. It's style over substance, perception over reality—everywhere you look. Success, or at least the appearance of success, becomes more important than anything else. And we allow our feelings of personal significance and worth to be shaped by it. I think that's why so many guys have so much trouble when they leave the game of football. They don't feel they have the status they once enjoyed, so it's hard for them to find significance in anything else they might do. Once the status they enjoyed on the football field has evaporated, they feel worthless. Of course, this quest for significance plagues men in all walks of life, not just in football.

Many young men (and even some older men) are really into the kind of car they drive and the brand of clothes they wear. Again, it's the idea that we somehow derive status from these things, with style being the key. Somewhere we've lost the concept that respect comes from appreciating who a person is inside and what he is truly all about. We don't respect the man; we respect what he does or what he has.

The real danger here is that choosing style over substance keeps us from valuing those things that truly do have worth. Being a good parent, being a loyal and committed spouse, modeling proper behavior for others, mentoring the less fortunate—these things may not give us status in today's world, but they are important to God.

It was refreshing for me to see a guy like Franco Harris ride his bicycle to work when I played with the Steelers. Or to watch so many of our guys today who volunteer at the local high schools as tutors or assistant coaches. These guys aren't concerned about image, but instead focus on significance and making a difference.

Substance or style—the choice is clear if we want to live the significant lives we were meant to live.

CHAPTER 19

PRIORITIES

If people concentrated on the really important things in life, there'd be a shortage of fishing poles.
  DOUG LARSON

NOWHERE IN OUR LIVES is the tension greater than in the area of setting the priorities that matter most.

And nothing is tougher than looking in the mirror and seeing all the mistakes we've made. Yet the complete story of our lives is not fully written; change is still possible, and we can still take control of our priorities.

Near the end of his life, Solomon, the king of Israel and a man with power, intelligence, talents, pleasures, and riches beyond compare, put it this way:

> *I observed everything going on under the sun, and really,*
>   *it is all meaningless—like chasing the wind.*
> *So what do people get in this life for all their hard work*
>   *and anxiety?*

What do people get for all their hard work under the sun?
"Everything is meaningless," says the Teacher, "completely
meaningless!" ECCLESIASTES 1:14; 2:22; 1:3; 1:2

Solomon says that to live a life seeking worldly things is like "chasing the wind." He clearly tells us, from his own experience, that life rooted solely in worldly values and riches is "completely meaningless." It is empty and will not satisfy.

And at the end of his life, after all of his experiences, Solomon wrote this:

> *Don't let the excitement of youth cause you to forget your*
> *Creator. Honor him in your youth before you grow old*
> *and say, "Life is not pleasant anymore." Remember him*
> *before the light of the sun, moon, and stars is dim to your*
> *old eyes, and rain clouds continually darken your sky. . . .*
> *Fear God and obey his commands, for this is everyone's*
> *duty. God will judge us for everything we do, including*
> *every secret thing, whether good or bad.*
>
> ECCLESIASTES 12:1-2, 13-14

Solomon's answer to a meaningful, fulfilling life is God; yet, even though Solomon was "successful," he never fully lived the life he was meant to live.

Too many men I have known live lives seeking fame, fortune, recognition and rewards, comfort and material things, and financial security. Their priorities begin there, and—since those things don't tend to leave time for anything else—they usually end there.

Yet on their deathbeds, these men wouldn't ask their bankers to come to their bedside, or to see all the plaques that adorned their office walls or the trophies gathering dust on their shelves. No, all of a sudden those things don't seem to matter—they don't seem to have the value they once did. Instead, at the end of their lives, these men ask for their families and others who are important to them; sadly, the people who have been there all along were not a high priority to them when they were healthy.

In the last ten years, I have lost my mother, my father, and my oldest son. As a result of my son's death, I've talked to hundreds of parents who have also lost children and to hundreds of kids who have lost siblings. Everyone I speak with feels just as I do: when you lose loved ones, no matter how old they are, you always wish you had more time to spend with them. I spent forty-six years with my mom, forty-eight with my dad, and eighteen with my son. I am grateful for the memories that I have—they were great years and happy times—but I still wish there had been more. But *we never know for sure how long God will give us with the people we love.* Sometimes it's only weeks. It doesn't always seem fair, but I think God uses those times to remind us not to take life and love for granted. He wants us to keep our priorities in order. I tell our players all the time that even though we put a lot of time and hard work into preparing for games, and as great as it feels to win, they should never let their work come before their families. If they do, I know someday they'll regret it.

The sad truth is that for too many of us, this is the story of our lives. But it doesn't have to be the end of your story. Yes, shifting your priorities will require some changes in your life, but in the end it will be more than worth it.

Making a change begins with the principles that Solomon learned late in his life.

A life centered on Christ, one that "chases after God," will not only help to free us from being preoccupied with our success, our careers, and our finances—all of which Solomon says is "chasing the wind"—but it also will redirect our focus so that we can learn to embrace the priorities that truly matter.

Coach Tom Landry pointed out that before he began to follow Christ, football was his number one priority; it was his god. His wife and family were somewhere down the list, though he was not sure where. After all, he was earning a living and supporting them—at least financially. However, after he began to walk in a personal relationship with Jesus Christ, he began to redefine his priorities. Next to his relationship with Christ, his family became most important. He continued to excel in coaching football, but it was no longer his number-one priority. He wasn't sure which number priority it was, but he made sure that it was always below the priorities of his faith and his family.

We have all missed too many memories and moments in our lives because of poorly ordered priorities. But even so, it's never too late to set things straight and begin to enjoy God's blessings that are all around us. Maybe it's in the beauty of a sunset or the wrinkled face of a newborn baby. It might be in the trusting laugh of a child or in the love we feel for our adult children, or even in the "second chance" God gives us through our grandchildren.

So how do you begin to set the right priorities for your life against the pull of the things the world says are important? It's not easy, but it's absolutely essential if you want to make sure you don't miss the things that matter most.

Start here: "Seek first his kingdom."[12] Take a few moments to be quiet and spend time with God. He will lessen your worries about tomorrow and release you from the breathless pace of the world's "urgent" priorities.

Dedicating a few hours of your time to the priorities God has entrusted to you may not seem significant right now, but *to those who need you*, it could make all the difference in their lives, and in yours.

---

[12] Matthew 6:33, NIV

CHAPTER 20

BEING VERSUS DOING

Insist upon yourself. Be original.
RALPH WALDO EMERSON

I NEVER ONCE HEARD CHUCK NOLL say that his value as a person was lessened because we were losing games. When he retired from football, he didn't lose his identity—because his job didn't define who he was.

In our society, this struggle between *being* and *doing* starts early and is often innocently encouraged. We ask our children what they want to be when they grow up, which really means what they want to *do*. If they love animals, we're not surprised when they tell us they want to be veterinarians.

Some children aspire to be bankers, or professional athletes, or the next American Idol, or an Olympic gold-medal winner. Maybe they want to make lots of money, or live in a big house, or have more cars than they can drive at one time. Great dreams—but they are all related to *doing*, not *being*.

Those dreams tell us nothing about who our children are, or want to be, inside—what their values and priorities are—those things that will guide them through all of the things they will *do*.

I believe we all struggle with this, but it seems to me that it may even be a greater challenge for men. That may simply be because I *am* a man and have struggled with this trap as much as any. That's my disclaimer.

Men feel pressured to tie their personal value to their career. Paul talks about the fruit of the Spirit in Galatians 5:22-23—"love, joy, peace, patience, kindness, goodness, faithfulness, gentleness, and self-control." Yet we rarely embrace these inner qualities because they don't seem to fit within the world of competitive sports or business. Too often, we believe that a man's value is determined solely by his achievements and measured against the standards of a world that pays homage to winning.

Unfortunately, many of our players feel this pressure as well—deriving their value from what they do and what they accomplish. They confuse what they do for a living with who they really are inside. Once they're done with football, they aren't sure who they are. For better or worse, they have the rest of their lives to figure it out.

Sadly, for better or worse doesn't always apply to their marriages. A staggering number end in divorce. My guess is that many of the players don't have that clear sense of self when they're done playing football, compounded by the fact that their wives may have fallen in love with their husband's high-profile role and lifestyle. Whatever the case, their careers have come to define them, and when they are no longer involved in football, they simply don't know who they are deep down inside.

A negative job review, or worse yet, getting fired, can be devastating. I've been there. Though it is understandably traumatic, it doesn't have to be defining. I hope you'll never go through it, but the odds are that you will.

If you do, take a step back and remember that you're not the first person to experience this. Your career is not you. It should not, and does not, define *who you are as a person*.

Every day in my line of work, I receive performance evaluations, often by people completely unqualified to give them. Though I must admit that I don't listen to much talk radio, I decided long ago that I would analyze the criticisms from my superiors, players, assistant coaches, and even sportswriters for things that might be helpful. Trying to constantly improve means being open to learning throughout your life.

I also realize that I can't control what is said, and I will not let harsh criticism affect my sense of who I am. People are free to criticize all they like (sometimes they seem to like it too much, especially when I've done something questionable in a loss), but I don't let it negatively impact me. I know that I was created by God with all of my strengths and limitations. Somebody pointing out the limitations, real or otherwise, doesn't change my strengths or the truth that I am and will always remain a child of God.

Being versus doing—distinguishing between them will make all the difference in the lives we live.

CHAPTER 21

FOLLOWING YOUR DREAMS

Life's like a movie, write your own ending.
  THE MUPPET MOVIE

I RECENTLY READ AN ARTICLE about Michael Westbrook. Westbrook was a wide receiver from the University of Colorado, drafted as the fourth overall pick by the Washington Redskins in 1995. The interesting thing about the article was learning about how much he *disliked* football. He didn't like the violence of the game, the phony nature he perceived from the players, the pressure from the coaches and fans. He said that he continued to play because he was trying to please others and didn't give much thought about doing what pleased him.

A great deal of this book touches on relationships. Others do matter, and putting them first is often a critical part of being an uncommon man. We have a responsibility, either directly or indirectly, to shape and improve the world. But Westbrook's story illustrates an important point.

God placed certain things in your heart. He gave you passions that others don't have. Society may not value those things as much as you do, and people may try to push you into a career that pleases their desires, but at some point, you need to answer the call that God has placed upon you and you alone. You have gifts, abilities, and dreams that no one else has. The things that excite you may not excite me, and that's great. Together we make up the tapestry of humanity. Just make sure that you follow those dreams—the ones that God placed within *your* heart—so that together we can create something beautiful.

I wrote a children's book in which I told the story of my younger brother, Linden. He had a different dream than I had, and we have different careers now, but we're both blessed to be doing what we enjoy. It didn't happen in quite the overnight way that the four-year-old readers of that book might think, but the general story line is true.

Linden was a bright kid, but had trouble committing himself to academics—he preferred to make his classmates laugh. He also felt pressure because people were telling him that he needed to follow me into athletics. I think he enjoyed sports, but he wasn't excited about them the way I was. Finally, he was able to focus on something he wanted to do: dentistry. He was an above-average student in high school, but he blossomed into an outstanding student at Grand Valley State and then in dental school at the University of Minnesota—once he had a dream to pursue. He had finally connected with the passion that God had placed within his heart.

A Positive Dream

John Ondrasik, the one-man music group confusingly named "Five for Fighting" because of his passion for hockey, began a Web site called WhatKindofWorldDoYouWant.com. The site is based on the premise that we all have things we'd like to change about society or our world, but often we stop at complaining. His charge to visitors of the site is to imagine what the world would look like if they could reinvent it the way they wanted. It's a great exercise, and one that causes people to think positively—not simply to rail against things they don't like, but to figure out how to change them. John's goal has been to get people to think outside of themselves. Though the site also offers visitors the opportunity to make donations to organizations that are tackling issues like poverty and autism, John has said that he's hoping people will realize that there is more to giving than writing a check. "Giving has been a selfish enterprise for me," he told me. "The way the world works, when I give, ultimately I end up giving to myself."

On the Web site, people can share in John's vision by uploading videos of themselves answering the question, "What kind of world do you want to live in?" Each video clip is associated with a charity, and about $1 is donated to the charity every time the clip is viewed. (Of course, individuals and groups can also make separate donations, either to a specific charity or to be divided among them.) John's introductory video clip charges viewers to follow through on those dreams, think outside the box, and figure out how to impact someone else's life for the better. And then another person, and another, and another.

Whether it is the high school graduation rate in Indianapolis or childhood diseases or people huddled in their cardboard-box homes when a hurricane hits, we all have a passion in our heart and a dream in our soul.

A Frog's Integrity

Our children love the film *The Muppet Movie*, which is all about integrity—the integrity of a frog named Kermit. He leaves the swamp to go to Hollywood at the urging of a talent agent, who promises he can become rich and famous. So Kermit sets his face toward Hollywood, not to be rich and famous but to follow the dream in his heart to "make millions happy." He makes a promise to himself and to the dream. The movie is the story of his journey to fulfill that promise.

At every turn along the way, he is approached by Doc Hopper, an entrepreneur seeking a "spokesfrog" for his chain of frog leg restaurants. Each time, Kermit refuses the offer of easy wealth, intent on fulfilling his dream.

At a critical juncture of the film, their broken-down Studebaker has caused Kermit and all who have joined him along the way to come to a grinding halt in the desert. Kermit is downcast, his dream seems lost, and the integrity that has carried him to this point is on the wane. A second Kermit—his conscience, perhaps—appears on the screen, and Kermit begins speaking to himself as he struggles with his emotions and what to do at this bump in his journey.

He feels guilty, believing that he has let everyone down. He is miserable and feeling sorry for himself. His conscience points out that he would also be miserable if he had stayed in the swamp, never setting out in pursuit of the dream; but he's now worried that in addition to his struggles in the desert, he has brought misfortune upon "a lady pig, a bear and a chicken, a dog, a thing, whatever Gonzo is. He's a little like a turkey."

Kermit then realizes that the main person he made his initial promise to was himself. He set out to accomplish something bigger than himself, and the others came because they believed in the dream. Remember, the reason Kermit was going to Hollywood in the first place was to follow his dream of "making millions happy." Whether he or Jim Henson, the creator of *The Muppet Movie*, realized it or not, Kermit set out to do "God things," to fulfill a promise and a dream that God would honor, that God would smile upon.

"To make millions happy." Kermit's integrity and the integrity of the dream required that Kermit stay the course. And at the end of that scene, Kermit comes to that realization.

But the conversation he has with himself when his car is broken down in the desert rings true on other levels as well. We will always have doubts. Nothing in life is easy, and we will second-guess our quest at critical times. Wherever we aren't seems preferable to where we are—we forget that it was a swamp.

Look, things change. Life throws us curveballs. Some days it feels like we're facing blitz after blitz. People walk out of our lives or let us down. Things get confusing, loved ones misunderstand us, and relationships become tense. Fear comes and grasps us by the back of the neck, ready to carry us off and away from our dreams. And it often happens when our cars blow up in the desert, or our lives take detours that we didn't plan for, or we get pummeled by disappointments, heartaches, and tragedies. But through it all, the dreams that God put in your heart never change. Your integrity—your promise to yourself—demands that you step up and follow those dreams to a better place, to pick yourself up yet again and push on.

Follow your dreams.

CHAPTER 22

CREATING BALANCE

For disappearing acts, it's hard to beat what happens to the eight hours supposedly left after eight of sleep and eight of work.
Doug Larson

I CAN GET A GREAT DEAL DONE the day before we're headed out on vacation.

It's a pretty remarkable phenomenon, that ability that we all have to ensure that we get a week's worth of productivity done ahead of time so that we can leave the office with a clear desk and a clear conscience. We've got our list of things to work through, and during the day—check, check, check—we move down the list, crossing things off.

I'm not sure that it's anything more than a specific example of self-discipline. Self-discipline is what Lauren and I are trying to teach our children, and it's a part of why I prefer to give our players as much latitude as possible. We are better as a team, and they are better as people, when they can learn to govern themselves and remain accountable to themselves and the mission of the team. It's really an issue of self-control.

I struggle with administering discipline, especially when it comes to disciplining my children. I want to correct their behavior, but more than that, I want them to see that there are negative consequences for certain actions so they can begin to discipline themselves. That's the ultimate goal. The way in which I instill discipline—passing it down so they will see the value in being reliable and learning from consequences—is important. I try to achieve a balance so that I get their attention without disciplining so harshly that it overwhelms the lesson or turns them against me. It's not always easy to strike that proper balance.

I wrestle with maintaining that same balance with our players. Just as with my family, our players sometimes do things that require discipline. I am then forced to determine how best to respond. If their actions are too detrimental to the team or if they demonstrate a pattern of bad judgment or problem behavior, then I probably will consider releasing the player. When possible, however, I prefer to stop short of that remedy since my job is to help our team improve and help each player get better, on and off the field. If I feel a player is trying to follow our rules, and if our staff can continue to work with that player without jeopardizing the well-being of the team, I want to keep him and help him develop.

My parents both had that ability to strike a balance between the level of punishment and the lesson to be learned. From them I learned that every situation was unique, but that I would face consequences for every wrong action. Even when I was mad about the punishment, deep down inside I still understood that they wanted the best for me and were trying to teach me something that would help me in the long run. I had to accept the punishment, learn, and grow from it. They tailored our punishments to each of our personalities in order to make sure that they got through to us if we didn't meet their expectations. For me, that usually meant the loss of privileges, often involving sports. Instead of being able to go outside, I might have had to stay in and do jobs around the house. I enjoyed the freedom of doing the things that I wanted to do, so losing that privilege was painful. And very effective.

I still remember the talks. "When you can control yourself like an adult and do the things that you are expected to do, then you will be trusted and allowed to do the things that you want to do."

Creating Balance in Your Life

It's really no different once you become an adult, except that you need to be able to control yourself without the direct influence of others, like your parents. No matter what age you are, the same premise my parents taught me holds true: when you can learn to discipline yourself to do what you need to do, you will be allowed to do what you want to do. For most young people, a light will go on at some point as they reach this state of understanding. Our goal is to help that light come on, whether for our children or NFL players.

People often ask how it is that even though I am not a "disciplinarian," our team plays in such a disciplined manner. I think it is because of our desire to pay attention to details and not take anything for granted. We ask players to do their jobs exactly as they should be done and to take ownership for doing them well. Doing things the right way and following through on what you are supposed to do is the difference between being a championship team and being a mediocre one. Reaching those different personalities in the way they can understand, while at the same time helping them to grow as people and learn to discipline themselves, is a necessary skill in coaching. It's very similar to my parents' approach to teaching.

That is how I have been able to create margins—those allocations of time reflecting a commitment to the proper priorities—in my life and strike a balance between the things I have to do and those I want to do. I strive to manage my time so that when the day's responsibilities are complete, I can head home.

To me, "balance" cannot be achieved simply by walking out the door at a set time or by scheduling a certain number of family activities. Rather, it is a function of our preparation and performance in those realms that we are seeking to balance, measured against our prescribed priorities.

In other words, if I work hard and get my work done, I can go home knowing that I have given my employer my best. If I am diligent when I am at home about being present for Lauren and my children, then I can leave with a clear conscience and right relationships when it is time to go back to the office.

The two biggest obstacles I have seen to creating margins in our lives are poor time management and workaholism. The former keeps you from ever feeling like you can allow yourself to leave the office, while the latter is a function of misaligned priorities, a distorted self-image, or some combination of both.

I know many men who have professional achievement as their main priority: climbing the corporate ladder all the way to the top. For some of these men, it probably flows from a sense that this will make them more valuable as men—or at least *seem* more valuable to themselves and others. They see themselves in terms of the respect, the status, or possibly the power that they hope to achieve through the job. Still others probably have an inadequate and unfinished image of themselves, and they believe—subconsciously at times—that more work helps them to be complete. They see themselves as the determined, diligent, committed worker, and therefore spend too many hours at the office trying to fulfill that image they have created.

I coached several years at an NFL club with a young man who had a young and growing family. He wasn't focused on the status of the position, and I think he really enjoyed the time that he was at home, although by the time he finally arrived there, night after night, most everyone was already in bed asleep. Our general manager and I did everything we could to encourage and persuade him to go home at an earlier hour—we asked him, ordered him, cajoled him, and so on. The only thing we didn't try was to threaten him. Any gains we thought we had achieved for him and his family were temporary. Whenever neither of us were there to usher him out the door, we'd later learn that he had stayed late again. I finally realized what the young coach's issue was—his image of being a solid, stable provider for his family was someone who worked long hours. His father had been an NFL assistant coach for thirty years, and he had always left home early and come home late, working through holidays and missing special events. Without realizing it, our coach was imitating his father and his behavior by staying at the office. As for me, I hope that I'm getting home enough that my children know that family comes before work.

Some men use the office as an escape from their families. To those, I say, have some guts. Make some changes. Go home and start restoring relationships one day at a time. There are plenty of good parenting and marriage materials out there. Avoidance doesn't solve anything; it merely serves as a temporary salve.

For the great majority, however, I would suspect that the inability to prioritize and work through tasks during the day is the single biggest impediment to having enough time to do the things they would like to do.

Doing things the right way all the time is the hallmark of a good team, and the cornerstone of a balanced life.

KEYS FOR ESTABLISHING A MISSION THAT MATTERS

1. Be aware that the world emphasizes style, but substance is what really matters.
2. Make a conscious decision to determine your priorities. If there are others who should be involved in the process (if you're married or engaged, for instance), sit down together and put those things in writing.
3. Be prepared to start making your actions complement your list of priorities.
4. Never confuse what you do with who you are.
5. Follow your dreams. Don't take them to your grave. Better to have fallen short than never to have tried.
6. Learn to discipline yourself so that you can begin to enjoy more of life the way you want to enjoy it.
7. Balance the priorities in your life—spend the appropriate amount of time and effort in each area.

PART VI

CHOOSE INFLUENCE OVER IMAGE

+ + +

I always wondered why
somebody doesn't do
something about that.
Then I realized that
I was somebody.

LILY TOMLIN

CHAPTER 23

RESPECT FOR YOURSELF AND OTHERS

Men are respectable only as they respect.
    RALPH WALDO EMERSON

DERRICK BROOKS LEARNED at an early age—from an involved dad—about the importance of showing respect to others. "My dad warned me about being a clown in class, but I kept doing it, and he came to school one day right as I was being the class clown again," Derrick told me. "He whipped me right there in front of my class. The moral of the story that he taught me that day is that it didn't matter how good my grades were if I didn't treat people well and have respect for them."

Hardy Nickerson became the first big free agent to come to Tampa Bay when he signed with the Buccaneers in 1993. The team was at the bottom of the NFL heap at the time, and it was unheard of for a great player, still in his prime, to *choose* to play for the Bucs. Hardy came from the Pittsburgh

Steelers, who were a perennial playoff team, and he took quite a chance by coming to Tampa as they tried to turn the franchise around. Almost immediately, Hardy became the team's defensive captain and a team leader.

During my first season with the Bucs, things started to turn around for us, and we entered the 1997 season with high hopes. In the opening game, at a critical moment when we were trying to protect a slim lead, Hardy received an unsportsmanlike-conduct penalty for getting into an altercation with a 49ers player after the play had ended. I was livid. We spent a lot of time trying to help our young players understand that they couldn't get foolish penalties and expect to win big games, so I brought Hardy to the sideline and asked him what happened.

"He disrespected me," Hardy said. I was dumbfounded. I asked him if he knew that we were in the process of building a team based on poise, character, and accountability to each other. As a team captain who had been with a winning organization, Hardy more than anybody knew what I meant as I reminded him of that. I asked him if he was willing to sacrifice the team—and our goal of winning—simply because his individual honor had been challenged or an unwritten code had been broken. I loaded the question to make sure that he got my point and to give him a chance to get back on board—quickly—so we could get him back out there. Instead, his answer shocked me.

"That's all fine until somebody disrespects me."

That was a defining moment for both of us, I believe. Hardy and I met later that week, and he came to appreciate where I was coming from when I explained that his attitude wouldn't work for a member of our team. As for me, it was one of my first glimpses into this psyche of respect and disrespect. If Hardy Nickerson, one of our most experienced and veteran players—a bright, thoughtful graduate of UC–Berkeley—thought this way, it was probably far more entrenched in the rest of our young men than I had realized.

A lot of people seem to believe that respect is a right, something they are entitled to upon birth. Instead, we need to recognize that respect is something you earn because of your character. I think, also, that we tend to confuse respect with fear. "I will make him respect me," I hear guys say all the time.

My power, my position, my stuff, my bling—these are the sources from which too many guys think respect comes. I'm concerned that when we do show respect, we're not even respecting the things that we really should. A generation or two ago, we respected honesty, being a good provider for your family, being involved in civic organizations and church, or being a good worker in any honest occupation. In my family, we also respected men for simply being good uncles. All of my uncles were interested in and supportive of all of us kids.

When Art Rooney Sr. was alive, he lived on the north side of Pittsburgh. As the owner of the Steelers, he would walk to the stadium every day, and people always looked out for him and his house, even as the neighborhood got rougher and many others moved out. Mr. Rooney never moved, but he continued to treat everyone the way he always had. Mr. Rooney knew everyone in our organization, from stars like Terry Bradshaw to the bottom-of-the-roster guys like me. He knew the secretaries and cleaning staff by name, and he made it clear that they were all important to the success of the team. Similarly, the people of Pittsburgh knew that he cared about them and their well-being, and that the Steelers were a community trust, cared for by the Rooneys. What he demonstrated day after day at the office, in his neighborhood, and in the larger community of Pittsburgh was an authentic and sincere respect for all those whom his life touched and who touched his life.

One year, the sanitation workers in Pittsburgh went on strike. As I recall, trash was piling up everywhere around the city except in front of Mr. Rooney's home. As it turns out, some of the workers were picking up his trash on their own. They didn't have to do it. They just wanted to pick up the trash for a man who had always demonstrated a caring interest in them and so many others. A man who had shown them respect.

True respect starts with the way you treat others, and it is earned over a lifetime of acting with kindness, honor, and dignity.

CHAPTER 24

SEXUAL INTEGRITY

*Instruction in sex is as important as instruction in food; yet not
only are our adolescents not taught the physiology of sex, but never
warned that the strongest sexual attraction may exist between
persons so incompatible in tastes and capacities that they could
not endure living together for a week much less a lifetime.*

GEORGE BERNARD SHAW

THE TALK.

We all know guys who are afraid to speak with their
children about sex and put it off as long as possible, or have
their wives do it, or just never have the talk at all. This is
understandable, because it's awkward.

But as awkward as it is, we need to be more up-front
about sex and its effect on our lives as men. I believe that
any sex outside of marriage—during or before—is wrong.
Most of us would agree that infidelity while you're married
is wrong, but I'm confident we wouldn't get a consensus on

sex before marriage. You may not agree with biblical views of sex outside of marriage, but I'm sure you're at least aware of the problems it's causing in our society.

There are three basic reasons behind my conclusion that even sex before marriage is a bad idea, which I'll tackle in order: it impacts our relationships, it can have physical consequences, and it goes against God's plan.

Emotional Consequences

I think the popular media do us a real disservice in this area. In many romantic comedies or dramas these days, a natural part of building any romantic relationship is sleeping together. And those movies and television shows are very effective, creating an emotional connection between the viewers and the characters so that we're actually happy for the on-screen lovers when it happens.

I think the reality is something quite different. Because of its intimacy—or what should be its intimacy—sex can negatively impact a relationship that might otherwise have had a chance to grow into a solid friendship and possibly a marriage. And that should be the goal of dating: friendship, and then, when you've found your soul mate, marriage.

Why sabotage the potential of this relationship or future ones for a few moments of pleasure? This falls into that same category that comes up so many times in being a true man today: learning to defer gratification.

As George Bernard Shaw's quote at the beginning of the chapter reminds us, sex does not assure that two people will grow closer together. Too often with young people, unfortunately, it only masks other problems in the relationship.

When I was in college in the 1970s, we had another popular philosopher: the rock singer Meat Loaf. In his classic song "Paradise by the Dashboard Light," he hits the issue of premarital "love" right on the head. The song tracks a boy and a girl on a car date, with the boy getting more and more interested in sex—right now. The girl refuses throughout, unless he promises to always love her. Finally, at the end of the song, he gives in and promises to marry her, pledging his undying love—to their regret.

> *I swore that I would love you to the end of time!*
> *So now I'm praying for the end of time*
> *To hurry up and arrive*
> *Cause if I gotta spend another minute with you*
> *I don't think that I can really survive*
> *I'll never break my promise or forget my vow*
> *But God only knows what I can do right now*
> *I'm praying for the end of time*
> *It's all that I can do*
> *Praying for the end of time, so I can end my time with you!*

Physical Consequences

Sex outside of marriage creates another problem for today's men: the issue of absentee fathers. Until you are married and ready to be a father, you are taking a chance that you'll end up being one of those dads who sends support payments and struggles to find quality time with his child. Sure, there are ways to be careful, but why take the chance? Only one method is foolproof and accident proof: just don't do it.

And it's more than just pregnancy. Sex outside of marriage has always involved health risks for both partners. We started with syphilis and gonorrhea in my dad's era, added herpes in my time, and now have HIV in today's culture. What's next? We don't know, but history tells us there will surely be something new in the area of sexually transmitted diseases.

Spiritual Consequences

We hear a great deal of talk that girls should stay sexually pure so they can wear white on their wedding day. Why isn't there the same focus on boys' staying pure? For some reason, there is a stigma on women who have a lot of sexual partners, but society seems to look at it differently when it comes to men. We've allowed ourselves to be fooled into thinking that it's acceptable because "that's what men do."

But the Bible tells us to "run from sexual sin! No other sin so clearly affects the body as this one does. For sexual immorality is a sin against your own body."[13]

God created you. Your body is valuable. Don't be casual in what you do with it—don't give it away.

Guard Your Mind

Finally, be vigilant with your thoughts and what goes into your mind.[14] Pornography is one of the largest industries on the Internet, which makes it easy for men to bring it right into their homes, where it will quickly gain a foothold if we aren't careful. Whether it creeps in through magazines, television, or the computer, the best way to avoid an addiction to pornography is to avoid the stuff altogether.

Addiction to pornography is just as real as an addiction to alcohol or other drugs, and it can be just as damaging. Like

---

[13] 1 Corinthians 6:18

[14] "Your eye is a lamp that provides light for your body. When your eye is good, your whole body is filled with light. But when your eye is bad, your whole body is filled with darkness. And if the light you think you have is actually darkness, how deep that darkness is!" (Matthew 6:22-23).

other addictions, it often starts in a subtle way. You don't have to find yourself at an adult bookstore or an X-rated movie to be tempted or led down the path. Today, there are so many avenues where we might find ourselves confronted with those impure thoughts. And even if we think we are mature enough to recognize them and filter them out, what about our kids? If I put the *Sports Illustrated* swimsuit issue on my coffee table, what message am I imprinting on my twelve-year-old's mind?

A couple of years ago, before a Monday Night Football game, ABC ran an opening clip in which a towel-clad woman was in the Philadelphia Eagles' locker room asking a player to stay with her rather than go out on the field. It was done partly to introduce the game but primarily to promote another one of ABC's programs. How many kids saw that spot and didn't have a dad there to explain that this was not supposed to represent reality, just the producers' attempt to "liven up the game"?

As with any other addictive substance, you can't be too careful with sexually explicit materials. The next time you're tempted to look, keep this in mind: I have friends who are involved in organizations that are trying to combat the global epidemic of human trafficking. They tell me there's a good chance that the person you're staring at is quite likely a runaway or slave, and that sultry smile is probably forced, hiding a life of incredible pain and hopelessness.

Just don't go there.

Dare to Be Different

It takes a strong man to be willing to follow this path of sexual purity, a much stronger man than the one who takes the easy way out and acts on what feels good at the time.

Joe Ehrmann is an assistant coach for a Baltimore-area high school. He was previously a defensive tackle for the Colts, back when they played in Baltimore. I had Joe speak to our team during a recent off-season because I really appreciate his refreshingly candid view on what it takes to be a man. He believes that one of the areas in which the world currently evaluates men is their number of sexual conquests. I think he's right.

And I think that's too bad.

It's too bad for the men and the young men they will influence, for our women and our young ladies, and for our society. The idea that men are somehow to be valued for their sexual prowess is not a new phenomenon; it has been with us for as long as I can remember. I see it with athletes on every level, starting in high school and continuing all the way up to the professional ranks. Male athletes are supposed to have a lot of women. It goes with the territory—and if you don't, people wonder what's wrong with you. It's hard not to buy into that way of thinking when you are immersed in such an environment.

If your convictions, for whatever reason, are that you shouldn't have sex outside of marriage, you're going to face a lot of questions, sometimes even ridicule. It takes a very strong man today to hold up under that kind of pressure.

Now, if we do believe that sex outside of marriage and viewing pornography are wrong or harmful, we've got to teach our boys and girls to see that as well—even if we once did it. I wonder if some fathers are hesitant to talk about this because they feel they don't have the credibility to do so. Maybe their backgrounds include sex outside of marriage, or maybe they're still stumbling with their own thought lives today. If this is the case for you, use those struggles and the lessons you've learned along the way to teach your children and help them avoid making poor choices. For example, a father may have smoked cigarettes at one time, but now he realizes they can cause lung cancer, so he quit. He wouldn't then turn around and let his children smoke just because he once made the same mistake.

If you aren't yet married, focus on positive relationships grounded in friendship, and stand firm in the knowledge that you are man enough without notches in your bedpost. There are too many reasons to wait. And being willing to be evaluated on a different scorecard is part of being an uncommon man.

CHAPTER 25

PLATFORMS

Do all the good you can,
By all the means you can,
In all the ways you can, . . .
To all the people you can,
For as long as you ever can.
  JOHN WESLEY

YOU HAVE MULTIPLE PLATFORMS from which to impact the world.

Too often we look to others to do that, or we decide that we'll wait until later. *Later, we tell ourselves, I'll have more free time. Later, the kids will be out of school. Later, I'll have more money. Later, I'll have more name recognition.*

Or we don't think we have the expertise to change what needs to be changed. No one would listen to us anyway. Perhaps the things that need to be done are too big, and we don't know where to begin. At that point, we don't even promise to do them later; we just throw our hands up and walk away. Maybe someone else will do it.

The father of a young man called me not too long ago. His son's fiancée had died in an accident, and he was concerned about his son. The date of the wedding was approaching, and the son appeared to be slipping into depression.

I called the young man, and we talked a few times over the next few weeks. I told him that it may not seem like it at the moment, but things would get better, and ending his life wasn't the answer. There were more people than he realized who cared about him whom he would leave behind, crushed. They would wonder what they should have done, what they could have done. He would leave an empty hole in their hearts. I wanted him to know how much people really did care about him, even though he was feeling this terrible loss. I knew the loss he was feeling, and I was trying to help him understand that what he was experiencing was, unfortunately, very real. Life is full of painful situations, but we press on and know that while the ache may always stay with us, God will help us push through.

We talked a few times and eventually got past the date on which he would have been married. Gradually, I could tell that this young man was beginning to push through the dark clouds to find a ray or two of sunlight. He still hurt, but I could tell by his voice that he was coming out of the state of despair that had gripped him following his fiancée's death. He thanked me and told me that he was going to be all right. "By the way," he said, "what is it that you do?" I told him that I was a coach. "Oh, cool," he said. "High school or college?" He really didn't know who I was.

The point is that he didn't care that I was anybody famous.

Whenever we spoke, I was just a guy his dad knew who had lost a son—and who cared enough to take the time to call him. I hope you see this point: people don't care who you are or what you do; they care that you care about them.

Losing a son gave me a platform I would never have sought, but because I had experienced this loss, and because this father knew of me as a football coach, I had a chance to help a young man. Was I a qualified therapist? Definitely not. My job does allow me to talk with a lot of young men, but I am just a coach, a father, and someone who has experienced grief and loss. When someone reached out to me, I was able to use my platform to make a difference.

I feel it's important that the players and coaches on our team understand the platforms they have in their lives. They are not unlike your platforms. Some are husbands. Some are fathers. All are friends to someone. All are teammates. All have platforms they can use to make a difference in the lives of those in their circle of influence.

It's also important that they realize the platform that playing in the NFL gives them in a world that places such a premium on sports. They have a chance to positively influence many people and mobilize them to change things in their local community and beyond. To lift lives that need to be lifted. To make a long-term and perhaps eternal difference in those they encounter along the way.

We all have opportunities to be either "takers" or "givers." Takers receive value from the lives of others around them. We all do that, and we should, to some extent. It helps us to become all we can be. Thank God for the people I've been around who have added value to my life. But we can't just take! We also must give or add value to the lives of those around us.

You may not be an NFL player or coach, a Heisman Trophy winner, or a Super Bowl champion. But you have a unique platform, one that can be used to impact lives that no one else can.

We've all seen fictional depictions of barbershops and the wisdom dispensed there, but there is enough truth in that to continue to fuel the stereotype. Growing up, I was mesmerized by the talk that went on inside my local barbershop. I usually went in on Fridays before my games, and in addition to listening to the other guys talk in the shop, I always enjoyed talking to my barber, Mr. Hampton. Mr. Hampton would always wish me well in that night's game and talk with me about school and girls and whatever else was going on in my life. He may not have called it a platform, but he certainly recognized the impact he could have on the men, especially the young men who came in thinking they were just getting a haircut. We always left with so much more.

As those environments seem to get fewer and farther between, we need to take every opportunity possible to interact with and be encouraged by other men, regardless of the setting. Remember—you stand where no one else stands. Sometimes it's behind a barber's chair. Sometimes it's on the field. Sometimes it's across the dinner table. You may never know the impact you're having on someone who's looking up to you because of your character, your life's work, your family life, or maybe just because of your friendship. People respect you, believe in you, and trust you. In those cases, and others that will come, you have a platform of importance in the lives of those you touch—for their good.

Use it wisely and in an uncommon way.

CHAPTER 26

ROLE MODEL

Don't worry that children never listen to you;
worry that they are always watching you.
   ROBERT FULGHUM

WE ALL HAVE INFLUENCE.

I am often contacted by people who ask me to call someone to cheer them up or encourage them during a difficult
time. Though I am happy to do that, I find myself thinking
that the person in question would probably rather hear from
the friend—the one who asked me to call—than from me.
Though there may be some momentary excitement due to
my celebrity status, that is sure to quickly fade, and I probably
won't have the chance to make a lasting connection. People
love to look up to celebrities, but how well do we really know
them? That being said, we all are role models to someone. We
may not want to admit it, we may not want to be, and we

may even feel as if we aren't worthy. But even so, someone is definitely looking up to us.

I noted earlier that Derrick Brooks is a great mentor to kids; he is also a terrific role model. I never had to worry about where Derrick was or what he was doing. I knew that he could be counted on to set a good example, whether it was in his academics at Florida State, on the field, or in and around the Tampa area.

We had a number of players like that in Tampa, and I still do with the Colts. When people hear that we prepare for the draft by considering character, I think some of them immediately assume that we are less concerned with winning and more concerned with having a roster full of choirboys. Neither is true.

In fact, the next choirboy we sign or draft will be the first one for me. We are, however, looking for tough—physically and mentally tough—guys who are good teammates. Character contributes to a player being a good teammate. And we're also looking for guys who will set a good example, on and off the field, for our younger players.

John Stallworth was a person like that with the Pittsburgh Steelers. John had joined the Steelers three years before I arrived, a wide receiver out of Alabama A&M. John played on Steeler teams that won four Super Bowls, was named to four Pro Bowls, and was pictured on the cover of *Sports Illustrated*. In 2002, he was elected to the Pro Football Hall of Fame. Even more important than these accolades, however, is that John is an outstanding person and was, along with several other teammates, critical to my development as a man.

When I arrived in Pittsburgh, I was a good kid who had been raised well and wanted to do right, but I was in a new situation—and new situations seem to make us more susceptible to peer pressure. I certainly was hoping to make the team and fit in.

John was a great role model for me at that time in my life. He was friendly and engaging and a lot of fun to be around at the stadium; but when practice was over, he headed home. He had a wife and a family, and as soon as he was done with work obligations, he wanted to be with them. Because I looked up to him as a player and as a person, I found myself wanting those things too: a stable home life and interests outside of football.

John never talked down to me about it or preached against the guys who ran the streets. He just lived his life, and I watched. And what I saw made a difference in my life.

We learn from many different sources. We model parents and friends, siblings and peers. We model television and movie characters.

That is why it's always important to see yourself as a role model. Right or wrong, somebody somewhere is watching you. I worry sometimes that as men, we take it for granted that the next generation is picking up the lessons they need for life. Every time we prepare for the draft and look at the backgrounds of players coming out of college, I see the difficulties they have. About 70 percent of the players who come into the NFL now didn't grow up with a father in the home. A lot of them struggle off the field when they come to us, and it's not completely their fault. No one has helped them prepare for the life they're now facing. What has been modeled for them at home?

Looking back, I see that one of the added blessings of growing up with two parents whose families lived nearby was the benefit I had of the positive influence of my uncles—my dad's brothers. If my dad hadn't been around while I was growing up, they wouldn't have been a part of my life, either. That would've robbed me of half of my relatives. What a loss that would have been.

Just about all of my dad's and my mom's families lived in the Detroit area. Many weekends we would drive to Detroit to spend the night with my relatives, and I must admit that when I was young, I didn't know who was on my dad's side of the family and who was on my mom's. My mom's parents had died when I was young, and my mom had grown close to my father's parents. My dad was close to her siblings, too, so my brother and sisters and I could never keep track of who was on which side. All told, I had twelve uncles who were around regularly, so keeping it all straight was a pretty tall task when I was young.

I used to love Friday nights with Aunt Rose and Uncle Paul. After a number of years, I learned that Uncle Paul, who worked at Farm Crest Bakery, had married my dad's sister. Until then, however, I had never known which of them had married into the family and which was my blood relative. They made it clear that it didn't matter; we were all family. On those weekends with them, we would go bowling, play pinochle, go to Tigers games at old Tiger Stadium, and stay up to watch movies on *The Late Show*.

Uncle Paul would ask me the same question every time *The Late Show* was coming on. "What do we want tonight? Do we want to watch a shoot-em-up or a love story?" He knew I would always vote for a "shoot-em-up" Western. We watched a lot of John Wayne, Steve McQueen, and Gary Cooper during those years, and we made a lot of memories.

I was able to see firsthand through my parents and their families how to treat my wife, how to relate to children, and how to treat others with respect. I learned the value of hard work and saw that all work was valuable. There was no difference in the way that any of my uncles were viewed, in spite of their varied professions. It was in those formative years, in those informal settings, that I learned that all honest work to support your family is worthwhile.

I'm not sure that we always see being a role model as part of our job description. We don't see the need to be intentional about it, or maybe we've become gun-shy about our own mistakes and shortcomings. I know some guys think that because they've made so many mistakes, they can't possibly be a role model for other men or boys, which is definitely not true. Some of the best advice I give to young guys is, "Don't make this mistake like I did!" When I admit that I've made mistakes, I am better qualified to explain just how bad the consequences can be.

You're not disqualified because of your mistakes—none of us is perfect. Thank goodness that the men who built into my life—my dad, my Little League baseball coach, my barber, my teachers—didn't think that way. They made themselves available to me, and I watched and imitated them and learned. I watched the older kids who were in high school when I was young. I watched them practice—they were fifteen, sixteen, and seventeen; and I was ten—and imitated them. Fortunately for me, there were some good guys at the high school, guys who weren't too self-centered to help the "little kid," and the things they modeled were beneficial to me. My guess is that they'd had some older guys who did the same for them. So those of you in high school, remember that there are younger kids who think you are special, whether you realize it or not. Be careful of what you do and say.

That's even more critical today as more and more children are growing up without a father in the home. If you and I aren't there to build into their lives, who is going to fill that void? What lessons will they learn? We have to be willing to be intentional and step into their space, whether it's spending time outside or playing video games or sharing in whatever their interests are. We can't afford to have a vacuum of positive role models. Remember, everyone is a role model, but not everyone is a positive role model. So be intentional and be a good role model. Our kids need you.

Some of us adults need you too.

KEYS FOR CHOOSING INFLUENCE OVER IMAGE

1. Earning the respect of others starts with the way you treat others.
2. Respect others for their character, not status.
3. Sex comes with consequences. Save it for marriage.
4. Be careful what you put into your mind. Keep yourself pure.
5. You have platforms that are unique to you. Remember that, and change lives around you.
6. You are a role model to someone. Be aware of that and be a good example.
7. Your past doesn't disqualify you from changing the world around you for good.

PART VII

LIVE YOUR FAITH

✦ ✦ ✦

If you read history you will find that the Christians who did most for the present world were precisely those who thought most of the next. It is since Christians have largely ceased to think of the other world that they have become so ineffective in this.

C. S. LEWIS

CHAPTER 27

ETERNAL SELF-ESTEEM

*You made all the delicate, inner parts of my body and knit me
together in my mother's womb. Thank you for making me so
wonderfully complex! Your workmanship is marvelous—how well
I know it. You watched me as I was being formed in utter seclusion,
as I was woven together in the dark of the womb. You saw me
before I was born. Every day of my life was recorded in your book.
Every moment was laid out before a single day had passed.*

*How precious are your thoughts about me, O God. They
cannot be numbered! I can't even count them; they outnumber
the grains of sand! And when I wake up, you are still with me!*

Psalm 139:13-18

SO MANY OF THE THINGS I have discussed in this book—
issues of respect, the facade of physical toughness, listening
to your parents and other authority figures, and not merely
doing what everyone else is doing—flow from a healthy sense
of self-esteem. If there were only one thing I could leave you

with, it would be the understanding that you were created by God. Before you were ever born, God knew who you would be. Your abilities, interests, and passions are combined within you in a way that has never been seen before.

You are unique, and that is good. That's the way God intended it to be.

God doesn't sleep, and He cares for you. As Jesus told the crowd that assembled when He gave what is known as the Sermon on the Mount, God takes care of the birds of the air and the lilies of the field,

> *And aren't you far more valuable to him than*
> *they are?*   MATTHEW 6:26

God knows your needs and your desires before you can even ask. He cares about you in your day-to-day living, in your excitement and in your grief, in your ups and in your downs.

Now stop and think about that for a minute. I don't know what you've experienced in your life or how those experiences have made you feel about yourself, but after reading those words—that *God cares about you in every circumstance*—do you think about yourself differently? I believe that God cares about all of us—He cares about me and about you.

I am concerned about kids who never come to believe that about themselves, kids who see themselves as cosmic accidents and haphazard, random events. If life is seen as accidental, then wasting my life, or taking someone else's, may not be that big of a deal. If a child feels that no one really cares about him, what do you think he begins to feel about himself? Our world has already gone too far in that direction.

I am troubled by a society that devalues life directly and insidiously and then markets that idea to our kids through video games, music, movies, and television. This, in turn, contributes to kids not realizing that life should be respected, nurtured, and protected. The summer of 2008 was the worst three-month stretch in the history of the city of Indianapolis in terms of homicides. Most of the suspects were young men, men who probably didn't see life as having value or as being something that God cares about. And with each killing, we actually lost two people: the victim, who is gone from this world, and the perpetrator, who may ultimately be sentenced to prison. Somehow we've got to reverse this trend, and I think it starts with getting our children to see themselves as God sees them.

Life is precious and should be viewed as such.

You were created by God.

CHAPTER 28

RELATIONSHIP WITH CHRIST

God blesses those who are poor and realize their need for him,
for the Kingdom of Heaven is theirs.
God blesses those who mourn,
for they will be comforted.
God blesses those who are humble,
for they will inherit the whole earth.
God blesses those who hunger and thirst for justice,
for they will be satisfied.
God blesses those who are merciful,
for they will be shown mercy.
God blesses those whose hearts are pure,
for they will see God.
    MATTHEW 5:3-8

THE BIBLE SAYS, "God blesses those who . . . realize their
need for him."

He wants you to spend eternity with Him in heaven.

It's pretty clear in the Scriptures that the way to ensure this is to recognize that you need Him. None of us is perfect, and because of our sin (falling short of God's standard for our lives), we are separated from Him. Without being holy, like God, we cannot be in a right relationship with Him—without something else occurring.

God has provided that "something else" in the person of His Son, Jesus Christ. God loved us so much that He sent His only Son to earth to die for us and take the punishment for our sinful nature, so that we could have a direct relationship with Christ and God. And all we have to do is desire to be in a relationship with God, understand that we can't do it ourselves, and believe that God sent His Son for us.

It's a free gift from God.

When we believe that in our hearts and accept Jesus Christ as our Savior (He died on the cross for us) and our Lord (making Him the number-one priority in our lives), then we are assured of spending eternity with Him in heaven.[15]

God Blesses Those Whose Hearts Are Pure

For Jesus, it's where everything begins. The heart. Our heart reflects to the world who we are—the inner character that we display outwardly. The quarterback of the soul, it guides the decisions we make along the way, and determines what we will leave behind us along the journey's path. Our heart sets the course of every day of our lives.

Jesus often spoke of the condition of our hearts. At one juncture, He was speaking to a group of religious leaders, those who were very careful to follow all the religious laws. His comments to them cut to their cores:

---

[15] See John 3:16-17.

*You brood of snakes! How could evil men like you
speak what is good and right? For whatever is in your
heart determines what you say. A good person produces
good things from the treasury of a good heart, and an
evil person produces evil things from the treasury of an
evil heart.* MATTHEW 12:34-35

When it comes to protecting the heart and keeping it pure, a few strategies have helped me. First, be careful what you put into your mind. The things that we dwell on or fill our minds with will often come bubbling back up whether we want them to or not.

Second, fill yourself with God's Word by reading it. There are a lot of great books you can read, books with positive messages that will help you. But I don't think there is anything that will help you as much as hearing directly from God, and that's what you're doing when you read the Bible. A lot of young people tell me that the Bible is hard to understand, but a modern translation can help. Most often, I use a translation written in the English we speak today, as opposed to the "King's English" of many centuries ago. My Bible even has study notes; Scripture includes enough challenging passages, so I'll take all the help I can get.

Finally, stay in prayer. Pray alone and pray with others, too, including your wife or girlfriend and your children. If you're a young person and your parents have never prayed with you—or haven't prayed with you lately—ask them to. This may feel awkward at first, but it will help bring you closer to God and closer to each other. Just remember that prayer is simply having a conversation with God. There are no rules or special words.

The depth and quality of our relationship with Jesus Christ are governed by the state of our hearts. It will reveal the reasons why we do what we do.

We need to make sure that what we do in church or in our community is done for Christ and not for our own prestige and acceptance. Are your prayer and Bible reading done simply to fulfill expectations or out of a sincere desire to find God, learn more about Him, and discover what He wants for your life?

In our relationships, the state of our hearts will reveal how we view those around us. Do we see our wives and children simply as "wives" and "children," associating them with all the usual responsibilities expected of us, or do we see them as special creations of God, His precious children whom He has entrusted to our care?

Do we see the burdens of friendships or the blessings of friendships?

Do we really believe that we were uniquely created by a God who loves us and walks with us?

The Bible says, "God blesses those whose hearts are pure," and then offers this great promise: "for they will see God."

CHAPTER 29

FAITH

It's faith in something and enthusiasm for something that makes a life worth living.
Oliver Wendell Holmes

WE DON'T CONTROL EVERYTHING.

That's difficult for us to admit sometimes, but I think that's central to some of the issues that plague us as men. I have young children who look to me to make sure that nothing bad will ever happen to them; I tell myself I'm doing just that. And I make sure they know that too. I am ever vigilant in protecting them.

I was tucking in Jade, my younger daughter, recently. We had said her prayers, and I pulled the covers up and bent down to give her a kiss.

She hugged my neck, pulled me toward her, and whispered into my ear, "Keep me safe while I'm asleep, okay?"

"Of course I will, sweetheart."

And I meant it. The reality is that we do all that we can, but our best efforts to control the world will always fall short. As one of more than six billion people on the planet, I can't possibly think I'm in charge of it all.

Therefore, I am summoning faith all the time: Faith in the belief that gravity will bring me back down the next time I jump. Faith that the pilot of the flight I'm on won't fall asleep in the front when I do in the back. Faith that whoever programmed the traffic signals set the other side to red when mine shows green. Faith that my children will come home safely when the school day is over.

We use faith all the time in football as well. Our Cover 2 defense requires a great deal of faith, and it can take players quite a while to get acclimated. Some never do. Because the defense is so assignment oriented, our players need to have trust and faith for it to work. They aren't allowed to freelance and simply run to the ball. They have to protect their areas, stay in their gaps, and "trust the system." They have to trust that everyone else will do his particular assignment and have faith that if that occurs, the defense will be effective.

It's much more instinctive to run immediately to the ball. It's that control thing we have within us. We want to control everything, make every play, be everywhere on the field. All players do that by nature, I think, but most can be coached to read their key and go to the spot that key tells them to go to, whether the ball appears to be going there or not. Those are the players we need. The ones that have a hard time believing that the overall defense is better even if they aren't personally right in the thick of the play really can't help us.

Offense requires faith as well. Peyton Manning throws most of his passes to a set spot before the receiver has made his final break. He has to have faith that the receiver will run the proper route and arrive at that spot when the ball gets there. The receiver has to have faith that if he runs his route at the proper depth and with the proper speed, the ball will be thrown to the spot where he can catch it.

Life works the same way. We can act like we're in control, or that we've got things figured out, but Jesus was clear that we are not promised tomorrow. Only God knows how everything will play out. And our lives will be more effective if we live according to His game plan rather than trying to take matters into our own hands. Paul wrote in his letter to the Romans that "in all things God works for the good of those who love him."[16] This doesn't mean that everything will work out the way we hope, but that God has everything in His sights, and that He will cause everything to work together for *His* purpose. In *His* time. Our problems, our worries, our sins, and our pain will all work together in God's time and for God's purpose.

And that is where faith comes in. Some things are beyond our comprehension. Some days—or years—it seems as if nothing is going right, and we get on a losing streak. Our teenage children don't listen to us, and they behave in ways that worry us. Our marriages may be going through a desert, where things just aren't what we thought they would be. Our coaches, our teachers, our parents, or our bosses may be acting unreasonably or treating us unfairly.

Even in the face of all those circumstances, God is there. God is with you, every step of the way, and He knows where this is all headed.

---

[16] Romans 8:28, NIV

As for me, I know that I can't make it through life relying solely on my own smarts and strength. Life is too tough, and too many things come up that I have no control over. Some people try to fool themselves into thinking that self-reliance is possible, but it really is foolish to think we don't have to have faith in anyone or anything else. It's also a lonely way to go through life.

And it leaves out the perspective of eternal life.

CHAPTER 30

PURPOSE

What kind of world do you want?
Think anything
Let's start at the start
Build a masterpiece
History starts now
Be careful what you wish for
Start now.
    FIVE FOR FIGHTING, "WORLD"

SO WHY ARE YOU HERE, anyway? Why are you wherever you happen to be at the moment you read these words?

I believe that God knew that you would be in the spot you are in right now, with the passions and gifts that you have and the platform that only you enjoy. I believe that the imprint you are meant to leave on this world is not accidental or coincidental. Your life has been intentionally designed by

God to have a uniquely significant and eternal impact on the world around you.

Think about that for a moment—your life has been intentionally designed by God to have a unique and significant impact on everyone you meet, and many you may never meet. What if we all lived our lives embracing that idea as true— what would our lives begin to look like? What would we attempt to do that we never would have attempted otherwise? What difference would we begin to make in the lives of those around us? What would our communities begin to look like? What would our schools begin to look like? Our states and our nation? How many of our children and youth who find themselves with no hope for tomorrow would suddenly begin to see the possibilities in their lives? What problems in the world that seem too big to resolve would begin to be addressed?

Though I do think there are things that each of us can do to improve ourselves and our lot in life, I believe first and foremost that I operate from God's grace. That grace is not a license to do whatever I choose but rather an understanding that despite my best efforts, I will fall short in my striving for God, and that's okay. Falling short is not the goal, but it's still okay. When it happens, I get up, dust myself off, and press on toward the mark.

And as I press on, I think that I am called to ask, "What kind of world do I want?" Anyone can complain, but I need to be prepared to offer thoughts on how I can improve—myself, my home, my town, the United States, and the world.

I read last summer that Indianapolis's public schools had the nation's lowest graduation rate for males—19 percent. That's fewer than one in five. My goal shouldn't be to cast blame but rather to determine what I can do to make an impact on that statistic, even if it's "only" for one kid. One kid, or one small group—and then another and another. And, who knows? As the word gets out about my one-man crusade, maybe someone else will join the effort. How many kids could we reach then?

We have all seen people less fortunate than ourselves, others who seem to have little hope for anything to change in their lives without some external intervention. We have all been saddened as we watched people in less developed countries die from starvation or disease for want of food, medicine, or other things that we take for granted. We may not have the full solution or the wherewithal to solve these problems ourselves—but we do have our own passions and abilities, and we can begin to make a difference today.

I believe my purpose is this: to serve the Lord and use all that He has given me to help others to the best of my ability. When I'm staying focused on that, it allows me to find the joy and abundant life that Christ promised, even if we don't win the Super Bowl or I don't meet every goal that I have for my life.

We're not always going to reach those things we really desire; in fact, failure may happen more often than not. But we can find peace and happiness in the knowledge that we're striving within our real purpose that honors God. If we're striving only for ourselves, then we'll be dissatisfied, always yearning for more, while the world waits.

Strive instead within a purpose—your purpose—that honors God.

CHAPTER 31

SIGNIFICANCE

Success is to be measured not so much by the position that one has reached in life as by the obstacles which he has overcome.
    BOOKER T. WASHINGTON

I THINK OUR SCORECARD IS WRONG.

I'm more inclined to agree with Chuck Noll's way of thinking: that our success on Sundays wasn't always measured by the stadium scoreboard. There were games in which we played very well but had fewer points at the end of the game. To the world, we were losers. Or maybe we played poorly yet won the game, whether through turnovers, penalties, or fortuitous breaks. To the world, we were winners. Chuck would rather have played well and lost than played poorly and won.

It's easy to fall into the trap of looking at the wrong scorecard. We decide that a head coach is significant, or a CEO, or a celebrity, or a billionaire. I don't think so. Those people might *have* significance, but it's not simply because of their position or resources. Significance is a much deeper issue than that.

Have you figured out what God has placed you here to do, and are you doing it to the best of your abilities?

Therein lies the answer to significance.

It's a liberating place to be once you figure it out. I was fortunate enough to coach a team to a Super Bowl win and reach what is recognized as the pinnacle of my profession. But it never has been an all-encompassing quest for me. Somewhere along the line, I realized that while winning the Super Bowl was something we were striving for, it was not going to make my life complete if we won—and not winning it certainly would not ruin my life.

Instead, I tried to focus at each stop along the way on those priorities I had already decided were important: being a good coach, learning enough to become a better one, and spending my free time with my family and in ministry opportunities. I wanted to win. I still do. God wired me to be competitive, probably you as well.

The best measuring stick of that competitive nature, however, is whether we are true to the call in our heart and act on that call to the best of our abilities.

God didn't create your life to be a series of accidents and coincidences. He knew before you were born that you would be where you are today. He knew that you would have the influence over those whom you do, and He already knows those you will impact down the line. Through it all, the legacy you leave—the imprint that your life leaves on this earth—will determine what your life on earth meant.

Nathan was giving a talk in Boston last year. He told the assembled audience about his experience in trying to become an author, or more specifically, trying for three years to talk me into writing *Quiet Strength*. He told of the ups and downs and despairs of the journey and the times when he thought he should give up. A friend along the way told him that until God clearly closed the door, he should continue with his dream. He did.

Finally, I agreed to write *Quiet Strength*, and a new set of challenges appeared. Some publishers wanted me to use a proven writer, not a first-timer like Nathan. Others were concerned about the tight deadline we had: thirty days to write it. Once it was written and delivered, we were forewarned that sports books generally don't sell that well and it would be difficult to make any best-seller lists. We were told how many books are written each year and that most sell fewer than ten thousand copies.

Nathan concluded his talk by giving statistics on the book, including best-seller rankings on the most prestigious lists (as high as number one), twenty-six weeks in the top ten, and sales of over one million. Then he tied these things to Proverbs 16:3, a verse that my parents had raised us on: "Commit your actions to the Lord, and your plans will succeed."

Nathan pointed out that the verse doesn't say exactly when we can expect success but that success *will* come in the Lord's time—maybe in three years, maybe longer. He also noted how God's plans are so much bigger than ours. Nathan's main goal three years earlier had been merely to *write* a book, without really giving much thought to how it might sell once it was published.

After the talk, a friend took Nathan aside and told him— lovingly—that he thought Nathan's conclusion was completely wrong. "You're using the world's measuring sticks—sales numbers and best-seller lists—to measure whether or not the book was a success. I watched you bang your head against a wall for three years; that, to me, is a success, whether the book ever came into existence or sold any copies at all," he told him.

My scorecard is slightly different. By the time I decided to go ahead with *Quiet Strength*, publishers were interested, so we knew that a book would result. However, we had no idea how well it would do. What God wants me to remember, though, is that in His eyes, success is measured by lives changed, not by total sales numbers.

God calls us to be faithful, not successful. He calls us to follow those dreams that are in our hearts and to pursue them with all our might. Sometimes they will proceed in ways that make them a "success" in worldly terms, but other times it may feel more like futility. Sometimes we'll be able to witness changed lives, and sometimes the only life we can see changed is our own.

God's scorecard is different from ours. He does want to bless us, but His scorecard doesn't use money or material possessions or fame or status. He judges by the state of our hearts and our desire to serve Him.

> But the LORD said to Samuel, "Don't judge by his appearance or height, for I have rejected him. The LORD doesn't see things the way you see them. People judge by outward appearance, but the LORD looks at the heart." I SAMUEL 16:7

Don't ever sell yourself short. God's purposes are greater than man's purposes. There is much to do and much that you are capable of doing. What kind of world do you want? Think anything. Just be careful what you wish for.

Start now to be uncommon.

KEYS FOR LIVING YOUR FAITH

1. Remember that you were created by God in His image, special and unique. There is no one else like you, and that's good. Accept a relationship with Christ as your Savior and Lord.

2. Watch over your heart. King David was described as "a man after God's own heart" (see 1 Samuel 13:14; Acts 13:22). David was focused on doing what he thought God would have him do.

3. To watch over your heart, recognize that you can't do it alone. You need to read the Bible and pray.

4. Know that you are going to fall short. Even David fell short—way short. He committed adultery and murder (see 2 Samuel 11–12). You, too, will make mistakes, but you can pick yourself up and press on.

5. Remember that faith involves a knowledge that God will make all things work together for the good of those who love Him, whether we can see it or not.

6. Keep seeking God's purpose for your life. Remember that whatever He has placed in your heart is bigger than you.

7. Key on the fact that God requires you to be faithful, not successful. If you remember this, you will end up being both—in His eyes.

EPILOGUE

Everybody can be great . . . because anybody can serve. You don't
have to have a college degree to serve. You don't have to make your
subject and verb agree to serve. You only need a heart full of grace,
a soul generated by love.
MARTIN LUTHER KING JR.

WANDERING ISN'T ALWAYS BAD.

Life is all about the journey, I believe. We pay so much
attention to where we are going or what we have accomplished that we sometimes forget to appreciate where we are
and how we've gotten to this point.

As I write this, Brandon Robinson is in the tenth year
of his twenty-eight-year sentence. After attending a chapel
service in prison, he accepted Christ into his life, and it had
a huge impact on him. He got his high school diploma, his
bachelor's degree, and an MBA while in prison. As part of his
community-service requirement, he has been allowed to go
out and speak to young people about the mistakes he's made

in life. He has a very powerful testimony. I have had him speak to our team not only about the dangers of drinking and driving but also about the dangers of falling into that lifestyle, and his talk has had more impact on our players than anything I could say. He has contacted the families of those five accident victims and been forgiven by some of them. However, no matter how hard he tries, he will never be able to forget the bad decisions that led up to that terrible night, and he'll never be able to erase their consequences.

Dallas Clifton is in the second year of his sentence, and he, too, is taking classes in prison. He hopes to go back to school when he's released. It's been difficult for him, knowing the amount of pain he has caused his mom and his sisters. Prison life is not easy, but it does give you time to reflect on a lot of things, including the decisions you have made in the past and those you will make in the future. And he, too, looks back on the rash decisions he made and wishes he could change them.

But life is like football in that once a play is run, you don't get a chance to do it over. You have to live with the results of that play. The only thing you can do is move forward and try to make the situation better. I really believe both Dallas and Brandon are going to do that.

Like Brandon and Dallas, we sometimes decide to follow the crowd, and the results make us feel like our journey has hit a dead end. Maybe you're worn out. Maybe you've hurt your wife or your children too much for them to even begin to open up to you again. Maybe you've headed into some form of addiction. Maybe you're at the pinnacle—and it's not all the fun you thought it would be.

Remember this: God has created you different from anyone else. You have gifts and abilities that I don't have, and

I probably have some that you don't. But we are both of infinite value in God's eyes, and both of us are capable of so much more than the world says we are.

We aren't supposed to be playing by the world's rules. The world has systematically changed the values of the important things in life, switching them with those that don't matter at all, assigning wrong values. Those things that are truly valuable have been discounted to ridiculous levels, while those things that are meaningless have been held in the highest esteem.

When our family is headed from Indianapolis to Tampa, we often fly Southwest Airlines. One of the fascinating things to me about Southwest is that they have been successful by going against the norm. They did away with assigned seating, ignored the major metropolitan airports, and cut their maintenance and training costs by having only one type of aircraft. In short, they didn't do it everybody else's way. At times, I'm sure Southwest's leaders felt like they were standing alone, telling their stockholders, "This will work. Trust us."

But it's okay to stand alone:

Don't copy the behavior and customs of this world, but let God transform you into a new person by changing the way you think. Then you will learn to know God's will for you, which is good and pleasing and perfect.

ROMANS 12:2

Be like Southwest. While everyone is racing around, trying to figure out how to get ahead in terms of worldly status and success, you keep playing a different game.

Start now.

Be *Uncommon.*

Q&A WITH COACH DUNGY

Part I: Develop Your Core

CHAPTER 1: CHARACTER

1. *When evaluating draft prospects, how do you find out about their character? Do you have a "character scout"?*

    We instruct our scouts to ask a lot of questions about behavior and character, not only of coaches but also of teammates, academic advisers, and other staff at the college. We have access to background checks, and our staff also interview the players face-to-face to try to draw our own conclusions.

2. *How do you specifically instill character in your family? How do you teach your children and allow them to grow into honor and integrity and learn to be accountable for themselves?*

    This is something Lauren and I talk about a lot with our children. We use examples from the Bible, Sunday school lessons, and life lessons in general. We try to have our children think about what God would want them to do in different situations.

CHAPTER 2: HONESTY AND INTEGRITY

3. *Have you ever had an experience in which being honest hurt you in the short run but benefited you in the long run?*

When interviewing for head coaching jobs in the mid-1990s, I was often asked similar questions by the team owners: Who will be on your coaching staff? What methods will you use to motivate and discipline the players? Will you treat this job as the most important thing in your life? Even though I knew the answers they were looking for, I wasn't always able to give them, and I know my answers hurt my chances of getting those jobs. But eventually God put me in the right job, with a front-office group that shared the same beliefs I had. With the two head coaching jobs I finally did get, I didn't have to try to live up to anything I might have said without really meaning it.

4. *How have you taught honesty and integrity to your children? your players?*

With my children, I try to teach honesty the same way my parents did: by stressing it. By rewarding them when they are honest and punishing dishonesty. By trying to demonstrate honesty myself in every situation. With my players, I always stress that they have to be honest with me. I'm in their corner, even if they make a mistake, as long as they're up-front with me. But if I can't depend on them, or if I find out later that they've put me in a bad position by not being honest, that will have severe consequences.

CHAPTER 3: HUMILITY AND STEWARDSHIP

5. *How do you encourage your players to demonstrate humility on the field (after a touchdown, a win, a loss) and to the media? Have any other teams or journalists noticed a difference between the Colts and other teams in this area?*

   We're fortunate to have veteran leaders on our team who demonstrate that type of humility. Marvin Harrison and Peyton Manning in particular come to mind. Because of their attitudes, and because so many of the young players look up to them, it makes it easy for us as coaches. We do talk to our players about being good role models for our younger fans, about being professional, and about not trying to embarrass our opponents. I haven't heard too many in the media comment on it, but I do get a lot of letters from fans—mainly parents—thanking me for the example our players present.

6. *How do you build a team that is focused on humility and stewardship?*

   I think you build the team that way by the players you select. We look for those qualities in the guys we bring in. But I also talk about it a lot in our team meetings. A crew from NFL Films was in our locker room after a big win against New England in 2005, and they recorded me saying this: "The Bible says that pride goes before destruction, so we want to make sure we remember the hard work and sacrifice that it takes to win in this league." I do try to remind our guys regularly of the responsibility that goes with the positions we have.

7. *Do you find it difficult to stay humble, especially as the coach of a Super Bowl–winning team? What kinds of things do you do to further develop that humility?*

No, I only have to look back on my career to realize that the difference between winning a Super Bowl and being fired is sometimes only one play or one official's call. I know in my heart I am no better coach—or better person—now than I was in 2001, when I was fired. I try not to go too many days in a row without reading my Bible. That's probably the biggest thing that keeps me humble. I know that the good things that have come my way are because of God's blessing, not because I have done anything to deserve them.

CHAPTER 4: COURAGE

8. *What scares you? How do you deal with your fears so that they don't rule your decisions?*

The things that scare me the most are the things I know I can't control, like health issues. I also have a fear for our country right now. I'm not sure we're headed in the right direction as a society, and if we stray too far away from the Lord, we're going to suffer the same consequences that other historical powers have faced. But I don't fear too much in terms of day-to-day living and decision making. When I do get in a situation where I'm apprehensive about something, I pray and ask God to watch over me and give me peace of mind. I try to remember that God really is in control of everything, and nothing in this world happens unless God allows it.

9. *Who are some of your courageous role models? How have they demonstrated courage for you?*

Dr. Martin Luther King Jr. stands out in my mind. He stood up against an immoral way of life when he was very young (in his twenties) and when the law of our land not only wouldn't protect him, but in many cases attacked him. But he had strong convictions, and he was determined to stand up for them, even though it eventually cost him his life. John Thompson, the former Georgetown basketball coach, was also one of my heroes. He had a passion for his players and wasn't afraid to speak his mind about issues that concerned them, even when most of the national media didn't agree with him. In 1989, Thompson had a confrontation with a notorious Washington, D.C., drug dealer named Rayful Edmond, who was generally credited with introducing crack cocaine into the D.C. area. Edmond's gang was believed to have committed over forty murders, and Edmond was eventually sentenced to life in prison without parole. When Thompson found out that Edmond was hanging around one of his star players, Alonzo Mourning, he invited Edmond to his office and lit into him, telling him he better not hear of Edmond being with *any* Georgetown players or Edmond would have to deal with Thompson. He took a huge personal risk that day, and his story made a tremendous impact on me. A coach that cared enough about his players to put his life on the line for them is a powerful example.

Part II: Love Your Family

10. *What would you say to someone who hasn't ever had a lasting romantic relationship and is lonely and frustrated with being single?*

Being single is not easy. We all long for that special relationship that will make us feel complete. Until we find it, it can seem like something is missing in our lives, and no matter how everything else is going, we may not be truly happy inside. The longer you search, the more it feels like love may never come. No matter what, though, don't give in to the false idea that it has to happen soon or it never will. Don't go forward in a relationship that you don't believe is absolutely right for you just because you're tired of being single. Trust that God already knows who that right person is for you, and will send that person to you in *His* time. It's tough to be patient, but that's where faith has to come in. And waiting for the right relationship to develop will be much better for you in the long run than plunging into the wrong one.

11. *You say that whom you choose to marry is one of the most important decisions in life. You also mention that it is important to ask God to show you who it will be. How did you know that your wife was the one? How did God show you that she was the one?*

It is your biggest decision because when you get married, you become one with your marriage partner. That decision will impact everything you do in life from that point on. When I was twenty-six, I hadn't had many serious girlfriends yet, but I knew very specifically what type of wife I was looking for. I wanted someone who was a Christian and had the same beliefs about life that I did. Someone who felt very strongly about family and would take those marriage vows seriously. However, I was beginning to wonder if I would ever find that right person. When I was introduced to Lauren, I was first attracted to her appearance, but it was in our conversations, in doing things together, and in getting to know each other that I began to know she was the one for me. There was no specific moment where God told me she was the one, but we felt the same about so many important things, and we grew to love each other as time went on.

CHAPTER 6: FATHERHOOD

12. *How did you and Lauren make the difficult decision to have the family move back to Tampa? What factors did you consider? How do you make it work?*

I lived apart from Lauren and the kids during my two first years with the Colts because we wanted to let our oldest daughter, Tiara, finish high school in Tampa. So we knew it could be done. We just felt that with Jordan's medical challenges and other things our younger kids needed, Tampa would be the best place for them. We thought about the amount of time I would be away from them and the strain it would put on Lauren to do so much by herself during the season, but we felt we could do it. It takes a little sacrifice from everyone, and I do feel bad that I'm not able to attend a lot of our kids' important events. But we talk on the phone quite a bit, and we e-mail and text a lot. We make sure that when we *do* have time together—weekends, vacation time, etc.—it's high-quality time. In short, we do the same things other families do when the parents have jobs that require travel.

13. *What has been your greatest challenge as a father?*
No doubt, it's balancing work time with family time. Trying to give my children the attention and help they need to grow. Also, trying to figure out the best way to nurture them and help them mature, striking the right balance between protecting them and letting them develop as young people.

14. *What do you think is the most important thing a father can do for his children?*
The most important thing is to let them know that you love them and that they can count on you to be there for help anytime they need you. I also feel it's important to set healthy boundaries. They don't always appreciate them now, but as they get older, they will.

CHAPTER 7: RESPECT AUTHORITY

15. *Now that your parents have passed away, what do you do when there's something you wish you could discuss with them or ask them about?*
I do have things that come up that make me wonder how my parents would handle the situation. More often than not, though, I can remember something they said to me in the past that gives me a clue as to what they would do. I'm grateful for the time they spent with us, and even though I didn't always appreciate it then, I'm

very thankful now for many of the lessons I learned from them. When I realize the impact my parents are still having in my life today, I am encouraged to keep trying to instill godly values in my own children now.

16. *As a father, how have you taught your children to respect authority?*

That's very tough. It's not our nature to want to yield to authority, but things will be much smoother for us if we learn how important that is. I try to model that for my kids by respecting authority myself—obeying the law and not being too critical of authority figures in my life in front of the kids. Sports is another area where we can get that message across by supporting coaches and talking about the player-coach relationship and how important it is to respect the authority of the coach.

Part III: Lift Your Friends and Others

CHAPTER 8: FRIENDSHIP

17. *How do you make time for friends with the demands of your work and job?*

That is hard. Because of the hours we work, it is tempting to limit any free time we have to family activities. But we have to try to balance that out. It's important for our kids to be able to do things with their friends, and it's important for Lauren and me to maintain our friendships with other people as well. This is easier to do with friends whose children are close in age to our own because then we can do family activities together. For that reason, we probably gravitate more toward people with kids. But we also have longtime friends who don't have kids at home anymore, and it's important to show our kids that good friends are friends for life.

18. *What is one of your favorite memories of the time you spent at the FCA coaches' camps with your friends? Why?*
We had a lot of fun times at those camps. I enjoyed meeting the many high school coaches and getting to know them. I really enjoyed the recreation time that we had, playing games with our kids, hiking in the mountains, and otherwise just having fun. Probably my favorite thing, though, was that Lauren and I would drive from Minnesota or Tampa and spend a lot of time talking with our kids and enjoying the scenery of the drive. Those hours in the car provided some great memories for me.

19. *How do you distinguish between being a "voice of godly wisdom and direction" for your friends and being judgmental?*
I think it's in how you do it. If I am talking to someone in love, saying things for that person's *benefit*, then I feel good about it and don't look at it as being judgmental. I think God wants us to speak to people, to help guide people in the right direction. If I'm just being critical because I don't like what someone is doing, if I'm not trying to be helpful, then it could be a problem.

CHAPTER 9: TAKING COUNSEL

20. *How do you handle conflict within the Colts organization?*
I think we have a good setup with the Colts. Because we have kept a lot of the same staff together for so long,

we've learned to handle things in a mature manner. All organizations will have situations in which there are differences of opinion or where certain personalities don't click with others. But we understand two things: number one, everyone's goal has to be winning and putting the best team possible out on the field; and number two, differences have to be settled within the chain of command that goes from ownership, to front office, to coaches, to players. If we're aware of those two things, then we can settle differences by submitting to the authority of those above us and keeping the good of the team in mind.

21. *When you deal with conflict, either at home or on the job, what do you do to stay focused on solutions and communication?*

The easiest thing to do when there is a difference of opinion is to look at it from *my* standpoint—here's what I think, here's why I think that way, and here's what I want to do. I try to look at why the others feel the way they do. Why are they taking the position they are taking? By looking at it that way, I try to see the benefits of what they're saying. In the end, I still might not agree with them, but it opens me up to looking at things in a different way and lets them feel that their position is being considered. And, above all, I try not to take things personally.

CHAPTER 10: THE POWER OF POSITIVE INFLUENCE

22. *What do you do to encourage your wife and children?*

I try to get my kids to try things they haven't done before. I do the same thing with my wife. I want to help them raise their expectations of themselves, to think they can always do more. There is a fine line to that. You have to give positive feedback to let them know they've done a good job, but also find ways to make them realize they can do more than they think they can. Especially with my kids, it's important to be there when they have disappointments. It's in those tough times that I have to let them know they're still special in my eyes.

23. *Who has been the greatest encourager in your life?*
My mother was the big encourager for me when I was growing up. She always looked at the bright side of things and always made me feel I could succeed, no matter what I was doing. She also constantly reminded me of Romans 8:28—"And we know that God causes everything to work together for the good of those who love God." And she stressed that "everything" includes our disappointments.

CHAPTER 11: MENTORING

24. *Who are some of your mentors today? How do they build you up?*
I used to have a lot of mentors as an athlete—older guys I looked up to, teammates I played with on the Steelers—and then coaches who helped me along the way, such as Chuck Noll and Denny Green. Now that I've been coaching for twenty-eight years, I'm one of the older, more experienced coaches. But I still have people who mentor me in life, including my current pastor, as well as several other men I've met over the years. I probably talk to the Vikings' chaplain, Tom Lamphere, more than anyone, and he has given me great

advice and guidance over the last fifteen years. But I have also stayed in touch with all my former pastors and call them when I need advice or guidance.

25. *How do you mentor young men? What steps do you take as you develop a relationship with them?*

I try to talk to as many young people as I can and help in the same ways that people helped me. Most of my advice is biblically based, and I try to get younger men to look at the future and focus on the things that are really important. In developing those relationships, I try to lend a listening ear and let them know that I care about them as people.

26. *Have you seen anyone come alongside your children as their mentors?*

My kids have benefited from a lot of mentoring relationships. My boys, of course, have been befriended by many of my players over the years, men who have been great role models and examples. A couple of the women who worked for the Buccaneers took an interest in my daughter Tiara and helped her when she was in high school. And the faculty at Spelman College was a wonderful resource for Tiara as well.

Part IV: Your Full Potential

CHAPTER 12: POWERFUL THOUGHTS

27. *What are some goals you currently have? How are you using positive thinking to help you accomplish them?*

My biggest goal right now is to have a tangible impact on young men in my community. I want to get involved in a hands-on way with helping boys become better students and better people. I don't know if that will be starting a program of my own or joining in with some existing one. In the future I'd like to do more with two organizations I'm currently involved in, All Pro Dad and Abe Brown Ministries, which is a prison outreach.

28. *How has your family benefited from positive thought?*
Lauren and I try to stress the same things our parents did with us because we know that a positive attitude is so important. Be optimistic. Be happy about the blessings you have, and don't focus on what you don't have. I think our kids have grown to be people who adapt well and believe good things will happen to them.

CHAPTER 13: EDUCATION AND ATHLETICS

29. *How do you set boundaries for your children as far as balancing athletics and education?*
We've always encouraged our kids to be involved in athletics, but we've *stressed* the importance of education. We require them to maintain good grades in order to play, and we've talked a lot about priorities. We know they enjoy sports, and there's nothing wrong with that as long as they do the job in their classrooms first. We tell them athletics are a privilege, as well as using the computer and cell phone, watching television, and driving. All these things depend on good academic performance.

30. *What advice do you have for athletes to prepare for life after their playing days are over?*
They need to recognize that those playing days will come to an end, and they need to think about that

time before it happens. Just like with playing football, they need a game plan and they need to practice.
They must think about what they want to do, and
then get a head start on the process by getting involved
in a program that will help them develop the skills
they'll need. Of course, it isn't easy to do this while
you're playing football at the NFL level, but it can
be done.

CHAPTER 14: CAREER, WORK, AND MONEY

31. *How do you set your office hours? Do you ever go home
because you need to, even if you feel there is more to be
done at work?*

I'm fortunate because I'm the boss and I can set the
office hours. During the season, we have a certain
amount of work that has to be done, so the hours
can be pretty tough. I have set the starting time so my
assistant coaches can take their kids to school if they
choose. That causes us to work pretty late, especially
early in the week. My staff members all have different
projects that they're responsible for during the season,
and I encourage them to go home when they're
finished. Don't stay because I stay or because other
people are finishing their assignments; when you're
finished, go home. I don't often leave when there
is still work to be done, but I don't stick around the
office much after I'm finished. If there is something
special going on at home or with one of the kids, I will
sometimes leave some work undone and come in early
the next day.

32. Are there things you would still like to change about your work habits?

I think we have done as good a job as we can in being efficient and keeping our hours to a minimum. We have a good schedule in the off-season, so I'm pretty satisfied with how I'm doing. One thing that does bother me, even though there's nothing I can do about it, is the fact that for six months of the year our schedules are so rigid—we don't have many days off, and we have to work most of the fall and winter holidays. So we have to make up for that in the off-season. But I have gotten to the point, after twenty-eight years of coaching, that I put a high priority on doing my work well and going home as soon as the work is done.

33. What would characterize the perfect job for you?

The job of being a coach is ideal for me. I like working with young men, I enjoy the mental challenge of preparing a team for a season, and I love being outdoors. I think God blessed me with the perfect job to fit my talents and personality.

34. You advise readers to not make choices based on money but rather on what they want to do. If money shouldn't drive employment decisions, how do you find a place where your passion and your ability to support a family meet? What if what you really want to do wouldn't allow you to earn enough money to pay the bills?

That's a tough question because as a young coach, one of my goals was to make enough money so that my wife wouldn't have to work outside the home when we started having children. That was very important to me, and earning enough money to support our families is obviously important to all married men. Taking a job that in the long run wouldn't allow you to pay your bills would not be acting responsibly. So I guess I would have to qualify that advice by saying that we do have to take supporting our families into consideration. However, I do think it's okay to make financial sacrifices in the short run to take a job that can benefit you long term. And I would always recommend prayer to ask God to give you opportunities in the field you want to pursue that wouldn't be a hardship on your family.

CHAPTER 15: GOALS AND RISK

35. *What kinds of risks do you encourage your players to take in order to achieve their goals?*

That usually involves our younger players and getting them out of their comfort zones. Many times we ask them to use different techniques than they're used to or sometimes to even play a different position. They have to take a risk, believe in us as coaches, and try to do things the way we ask.

36. *What kinds of risks do you take with the Colts as an organization?*

As the leader, I try to take calculated risks, but not unnecessary ones. However, there are times when I do, and they're usually times when I have a gut feeling about something. It might be about a player who most people think is too small, or it might be in hiring a young coach with limited experience. But for the most part, I probably take fewer risks for my organization than I do personally.

37. *What is the greatest risk you have ever taken?*

The biggest risk I took was signing with the Pittsburgh Steelers out of college rather than going to the Canadian League to play quarterback. I would have pretty much had a guaranteed contract in Canada with a large signing bonus and been able to play the position I had trained for my whole life. By going to the Steelers, I signed for far less money with no guarantees of even making the team, and I had to switch to a position I had never played. It probably wasn't the "smartest" thing to do, but it worked out for me.

CHAPTER 16: ALCOHOL AND DRUGS

38. *Do Colts players provide positive peer pressure for each other in the consumption of alcohol?*

Most of our veterans take the initiative to help our younger guys. I don't know how many guys we have who encourage their teammates not to drink at all, but we have a lot of guys who speak to them about not drinking in excess and being safe—definitely not driving when they have had anything to drink.

39. *What advice do you have for parents who are trying to teach their children to avoid the dangers of alcohol and drugs?*

Number one, set the example. The best thing you can do to keep your children from drug and alcohol use is to not use them yourself. You can also use the metro section of your local newspaper and keep track of all the problems that can be traced to drug and alcohol use. And you'll see plenty of it every day: auto accidents, arrests, health issues. Many times a picture (or articles in this case) can be worth a thousand of your words.

CHAPTER 17: FAILURE

40. Which of your failures has been the most difficult?
How did you overcome the negative feelings provoked
by failure? What made you decide to keep going and
endure?

In my head-coaching career at Tampa and
Indianapolis, my teams had the reputation of playing
well in the regular season but not in the playoffs.
From 1999 through 2004, we had six disappointing
losses in the playoffs. Then in 2005, we had the best
regular season record in the NFL and were heavily
favored to win the Super Bowl. We lost our first
playoff game that year, and it was pretty devastating.
Of course, the media revved up their charge that my
teams were underachievers in the playoffs and that
it must have something to do with my leadership.
After seven consecutive years of disappointment, my
resolve was definitely tested. Sometimes I wondered
what was wrong and why our regular season success
was not carrying over into the playoffs. But through
it all, I had to keep the faith in our system—not
only in myself but in our whole staff and organization. I tried to analyze what we were doing to see
if we could do anything better in the playoffs, but
I didn't second-guess myself. And I kept telling
myself that with all the disappointments, if we did
eventually win a Super Bowl, it would be that much
sweeter. In the end, I just believed that God had me
in coaching and that eventually He would give me
a feeling of satisfaction from my career, even if He
didn't give us a Super Bowl victory.

41. *In the world of sports, where it's all about winning and losing, how do you stay focused on the positive when you aren't winning?*

Winning is what we're judged by, but I try to stay focused on the other parts of the job. I try to concentrate on the things that are important to me—seeing my players improve on and off the field, preparing and practicing well, and doing everything I can do to represent our organization and the city of Indianapolis well. I know if I do that, I can then let the wins take care of themselves.

Part V: Establish a Mission That Matters

CHAPTER 18: STYLE VERSUS SUBSTANCE

42. *How does the concept of "style versus substance" make a difference in the lifestyle you and your family have, as someone who is wealthy and famous?*

Lauren and I are really making an effort to teach our children that who you are is more important than what you have and that material things should not be the motivation that drives us. It's hard because, due to my job, we do have a lot of material blessings, fame, and notoriety. We try to keep it all in perspective and explain to our children that those things could all be gone very quickly if our team doesn't do well. I personally try to set the same example my dad did—even though we can afford a lot of things, we don't have to have it all whenever we want it. We all want our kids to have a better life than we did, so my children definitely have more than I did growing up. But we do want them to realize that it should come through hard work and that we should always be thankful to God for what we have. More than anything, we're trying to teach them that although we've been blessed in this way, more than many of their friends, it doesn't make us better. The kind of people we are is more important than the things we have.

43. *Do you turn to a particular verse in Scripture to remind you to choose substance over style?*

Matthew 16:26 (NIV)—"What good will it be for a man if he gains the whole world, yet forfeits his soul?" You can have everything the world has to offer, but if your relationships to God and other people are not right, it will be very empty for you in the long run.

CHAPTER 19: PRIORITIES

44. *Has there ever been a time when your professional and personal priorities came into conflict, forcing you to choose one at the expense of the other? What did you do in that situation? Do you wish you had responded differently?*

The toughest decisions I've had to make have been with respect to coaching in Indianapolis and having my family live in Tampa. We did it for two years while my oldest daughter was finishing high school. This past year, we decided to move the rest of the family back to Tampa. There were a number of reasons for that, but ultimately we believed that it was best for our children. I still had the desire to continue coaching, and we had to make a family decision as to whether I should or not. There was definitely a conflict in my mind, and as I'm writing this, there are some days when I wish they were in Indianapolis with me. But we prayed about the decision, and we all felt good about it as a family, so I don't second-guess myself.

45. *Beyond attending Eric's football games, what are some specific examples of how you stay* there *for your own family during the football season, especially when you are living in different states?*

I try to keep Friday afternoons and Saturdays free for my family. Lauren and I used to make Friday night date night, but now that the kids are older we include them in our activities. We usually do something outdoors—bike riding, going to the park, things like that. We now have a video phone so I can talk with the kids and they can see me during the week. They enjoy that, and it helps to keep me in touch with them while I'm in Indianapolis. When they come up for the games, I take them to the team hotel so we can all stay in the same room. They think going to the games is like a mini family vacation.

CHAPTER 20: BEING VERSUS DOING

46. *How do you encourage your players to place emphasis on being versus doing when so much in the world of the NFL is performance based?*

We talk a lot with our players about what's going on in their lives and how they're doing off the field. We have a community relations department that helps them get involved in causes they would like to support in the Indianapolis area. We also have a chaplain who does team Bible studies and personal counseling with them.

47. *When did you struggle with your identity the most? How did you learn that being is more important than doing? How did you find your true identity?*

I've always felt pretty good about myself and who I am. My parents were a big part of that, because they emphasized that we should let our character define us more than anything else. My coach with the Steelers, Chuck Noll, helped me as well. He always said, "Football is not your life's work." What he meant by that was that you couldn't let your football career define you as a person. When I was finally done playing professional football, though, it was a little strange for me. It was the first time in my life that I wasn't an athlete or playing a sport. I also missed the camaraderie of being on a team, and I realized I would never be in that locker room environment again. But I knew I had a lot of friends outside of football, and by that time I was maturing as a Christian and understanding that God did have a plan for me—I just had to find what it would be.

48. *How do you identify yourself?*

I have thought about that a lot in my life. People today call me Coach Dungy, but I would identify myself as a Christian first. That's the most descriptive, and the most important, aspect of who I am. Also, growing up in the Civil Rights era, I have great pride in being African American.

CHAPTER 21: FOLLOWING YOUR DREAMS

49. Was it difficult to give up your dream of being a player in the NFL? Can you describe the process of going from that loss to discovering a new dream of coaching?

The hardest thing was giving up some of those teammate relationships. Though I would still remain very close to a lot of the guys I played with, there's something special about being on a team together and sharing those highs and lows that you can't duplicate anywhere else. I would miss the fun of being out there on the field and competing against the best players in the world, but I had always known that at some point I would have to move on. The biggest question for me was, "What do I really want to do?" I had a degree in business administration, but I'd never found a job that I really enjoyed. Once I got a taste of coaching, I found I loved the challenge of helping players get better.

50. You've won the Super Bowl. What dreams and goals are you pursuing now?

My goals now involve seeing how I can help our young people improve their quality of life. Especially our young men. I want to be involved in spreading the gospel of Jesus Christ, but I don't think it will be in a church setting. I dream of being involved in a program for boys that will give them some good, practical life lessons and also help them spiritually.

CHAPTER 22: CREATING BALANCE

51. *Has there ever been a time in your career when your life was out of balance? Who pointed this out to you, and how did you bring things back into balance?*

When I was in college, I was totally focused on athletics and going to school. I didn't focus on much else, including my faith. School and football weren't bad things to be involved in, but I needed to learn there were other things in life. I don't know if any one person pointed that out to me, but Donnie Shell, one of my teammates with the Steelers, was the one who helped me get back on track spiritually. By getting involved in the Bible studies and reading God's Word more, I was able to see that God had a lot of fun things to experience in this world.

52. *Why is it crucial to practice self-discipline?*

The best players in the NFL are the ones who really have self-discipline. Your coaches can go over a lot of things, and they can help players improve by working with them during practice. But the coaches can only do so much. The truly great players are those who push themselves and discipline themselves to do things right all the time, to be the best that they can be. It's the same way in life. If you have to have someone else motivate you, push you, and keep an eye on you to make sure you're doing what you're supposed to do, you will always be able to cut corners. The person who is dedicated and can discipline himself will be the one who succeeds most often.

Part VI: Choose Influence over Image

CHAPTER 23: RESPECT FOR YOURSELF AND OTHERS

53. Do you ever have to face disrespectful treatment from the media or other teams? How do you respond in those situations? How do you avoid answering in kind?

There will always be situations where you aren't treated the way you feel you should be. I've found the best way to get respect is to treat other people with respect. That's not always easy. When I respond to anyone, I want to do it in a way that I'll be proud of at the end of the day. Like everyone, I've said and done things that I later regretted. So I try to think before I speak or act, and when I don't show the proper respect to someone, I try to apologize—even if they haven't been very respectful to me. What is important to me is how I treat people and what kind of role model I am for the people who are watching me. That's more important than how the other person is treating me. And I can't say I've always responded the right way, but I sure try.

54. What kinds of things do you encourage your players to do to show respect for others?

The most important thing is to treat people the way you want to be treated, no matter who they are. That's really what I've done as a coach. I try to coach my players the way that I would want to be coached. It's the same thing off the field. Treating everyone as important and showing respect is not that hard. Just put yourself in other people's shoes and give them the respect and courtesy that you would like to receive.

CHAPTER 24: SEXUAL INTEGRITY

55. *What steps should a father take to open the door to conversations about sex and sexual purity with his children?*

    This is a very hard topic for most dads to take up with their children because we don't want to start them too young, and we don't always know what to say. But, like any other subject, just being open and honest with your children about sex is the best way. I think it's important to talk about what God has to say about it. We have to let them know that everything they see and hear is not necessarily the way God views it.

56. *How did you talk to your own children about this topic?*

    I have to admit, I waited too long to talk to Jamie and Eric about it, and I let Lauren have most of the early conversations with Tiara. Not surprisingly, when we did start to talk about it, they knew a lot more than I thought they knew. So I'll definitely make a conscious effort to start earlier with our younger children. But our common thread with all our kids has been that, yes, they will become attracted to the opposite sex, just as Mom and I became attracted to each other. Certain things are appropriate when you're friends, and certain things are appropriate when you begin to like each other in that special way. We talked about one of the results of sex being children, and both should only happen after you're married.

57. *How can a father teach his children to guard their minds?*

    Again, I think what we *do* is the best example. We have to guard our minds and the material that comes into our house first. Then we have to be diligent about what gets in front of our children. Information today comes to them in so many different ways, and we have to be particularly careful not only of what they see on TV or at the movies, but also what type of music they listen to, what they see on the Internet, and what kind of books they're reading.

Really try to watch the information sources that come to them. We try not to have them involved with too many things that aren't age appropriate. We try to know who their friends are and direct them to people who share the same values we do. This gets harder and harder as they get older. But we try to constantly remind them that good, wholesome thoughts are what they need to focus on. Keeping open lines of communication, especially when your children hit those teen years, is very important.

CHAPTER 25: PLATFORMS

58. *When you first became a head coach and a public figure, how did you decide how to use your platform for good?*
Fortunately, I had some time to think about that before I became a head coach. I knew I wanted to use that position to make an impact in the community, so I had to make decisions about what programs I wanted to support. I decided that my priorities would be Christian programs that would benefit families and children.

59. *As a coach, have you ever been able to use your platform to influence and shape the character of your players?*
I have been in professional football my whole career, so we're working with a group that is a little older, but I do—as Coach Noll did with me—talk to my players a lot about life, about community service, and about

being good citizens and good teammates. I don't think we have as much influence on our players as high school and college coaches have on theirs, but we try. And it is gratifying to have players come back to me later and say that something we said helped them to live a better life.

60. *What do you do to build uncommon players?*

I try to challenge our players to be uncommon. Not to take the easy way or the popular way. I ask them to be different, to be role models, and to do more for our community than just play entertaining football. The Colts organization helps them if they want to get involved in community service, and the NFL has programs to assist players in developing charitable foundations if they're interested. We have two men that serve as full-time chaplains to our team, so we're trying to help them develop in all areas of their lives.

CHAPTER 26: ROLE MODEL

61. *Who are some of your children's role models? How did you teach them to choose good ones?*

I know my boys look up to a lot of the players on my team. That's one reason I stress to our players what an impact they have and what a great responsibility it is. My kids were blessed in the fact that for so many years they had their mom and dad and both sets of married grandparents to look up to. The other place we encouraged them to find role models was in our church, and they found some great ones there. We always talk to our kids about who are good examples to follow and who are not. Lauren and I also try to spend time with friends who share the same values we have so our kids can see those good examples.

62. *Who has been your greatest role model in your coaching career?*

I studied a lot of coaches as I was starting my career. Obviously, working for Coach Noll for ten years made a huge impact on me, and I got to see more of him than anyone else.

Part VII: Live Your Faith

CHAPTER 27: ETERNAL SELF-ESTEEM

63. *When and how did you come to know God and how He cares for you?*

I learned about God from my parents and grandparents. Watching and listening to them helped me to understand that there is a God. But it was really reading the Bible and seeing for myself God's history in the world, His description of Himself, and His plans for the world that let me know that He personally cares about me. That happened in my early twenties, and the more I've read and prayed, the more I've come to feel that personal connection with God.

CHAPTER 28: RELATIONSHIP WITH CHRIST

64. *Has the way you think about heaven changed since you lost your parents and your son? If so, how? What difference does it make in your sadness?*

Not the *way* I think about heaven, but I probably think *more* about it now. I always believed heaven was a real place, but it is certainly more concrete to me now. I miss my parents and my son quite a bit. But I'm not sad very often that they're not here. I know I would feel differently if I didn't have a strong faith that I'll see them again in heaven.

65. *Do your children share your faith?*

I think they're a lot like I was at that age. They have heard a lot about the Lord and they know their parents believe in God, so they have that inside them. My hope is they'll continue to grow, continue to read the Bible and pray, and soon will know for themselves beyond a shadow of a doubt that God's promises are real.

66. *How do you teach your children to follow Christ?*

By living a life that honors Christ in front of them. By acknowledging Him in everything we do and by talking to the kids about the Lord at every opportunity. Most important, though, is letting them see how real Christ is to us.

CHAPTER 29: FAITH

67. *Do you ever find yourself trusting in your own abilities and trying to make it on your own in difficult situations? How do you get back to an attitude of faith?*

I have had a few times in my life when I've thought that I was doing things well and I was feeling good about myself. They were usually times when our team was playing well and I started to take it for granted. When I feel that I've got everything under control and that success will continue to come, usually the Lord causes some things to happen to remind me that it's not through my smarts or hard work that the success is coming. Sure, I know I have to work hard and do my job well, but I have to realize that God controls every-thing, and He wants me to remember that. And the times I usually forget that are the times I'm experiencing success. So those are the times I most need to remind myself to stay thankful and to stay humble.

68. *Have you ever experienced anything or encountered anyone in your career that has challenged your faith?*

When I got fired in Tampa, it did have an impact on me because I really felt it was the Lord's will for our staff to go there. I didn't think that necessarily meant we would win a Super Bowl, but I felt we'd have success, remain there for a long time, and do some things to impact the community. I guess I never thought of it ending, so when I lost my job, I questioned what went wrong. Did God just forget about our staff and our families? But I can look back now and see how He used even those trying times for good. I learned a lot from that experi-ence, and it made me a better coach—and probably strengthened my faith as well.

CHAPTER 30: PURPOSE

69. *What would you say to someone who feels adrift, like they have no purpose in life or they can't find it?*

They're probably looking for the wrong thing. They're probably looking for something to grab them—an occu-pation, a cause, or a station in life. Instead, I think we have to look at relationships, the primary one being a relationship with God. If you understand that He has a plan for you and wants to make it known to you, that's the first step. I know there are people who are Christians and want to serve God, but they still aren't sure what He wants them to do. In that case, you have to continue to pray and ask for guidance, and then trust your feelings. Let God use the desires you have to head you in the right direction, and then look for Him to open doors of opportunity for you.

70. *How did you discover this purpose in your own life?*
Once I got committed to serving the Lord, I felt He had given me the interest in football and the ability to learn the game. Although He opened some doors for me to get started in professional coaching at a very young age, I realized that my primary purpose wasn't to coach but to serve God. He was just allowing me to do it in a way that I loved.

71. *How do you carry out your purpose in day-to-day life?*
I try to think of ways I can serve the Lord wherever I am. I want to let my life show people what it means to be a Christian. I want them to see something appealing in me so I can tell them about the Lord. That's something that motivates me every day, no matter where I am or what I'm doing. Whether it's at work, with friends, or at home with my family, I try to always remember that I'm representing Christ and that someone may be attracted to Him or turned off to the gospel based on what they see from me.

CHAPTER 31: SIGNIFICANCE

72. *What do you tell your players about success and significance in the locker room after a loss?*
We're always disappointed in the locker room after a loss. In those moments right after the game, I talk about

the reasons we didn't have success that day and what we need to do to improve our chances to have success the next time out. I do this because that's where our focus is on game day—having success on the field. But there are plenty of other times during the week when I'll have the chance to talk about long-term impact and the fact that success and significance are totally different. We want to be successful on the field, and we want to win. Winning may give us some significance in the world's eyes, but it will be short-lived. There's always another champion next year. Real, true significance doesn't come from winning games or running a successful business. It comes from having a positive impact on the people around us.

73. *How do you guide your children to find their significance? How do you guide your players to find their significance?*
I try to get them to think about what they want to do to impact the people around them. You want to do something that you enjoy and use it to help other people. And if you're making a positive impact in people's lives, and glorifying God while you're doing it, you'll be very satisfied with your life.

ABOUT THE AUTHORS

TONY DUNGY IS the #1 *New York Times* best-selling author of *Quiet Strength*. He led the Indianapolis Colts to Super Bowl victory in 2007, the first such win for an African American coach. Dungy had taken eight of his previous ten teams to the playoffs. With this victory, he joined Mike Ditka and Tom Flores as the only individuals to win the Super Bowl as a player and head coach.

Dungy joined the Colts in 2002 after serving as the most successful head coach in Tampa Bay Buccaneers history. He has also held assistant coaching positions with the University of Minnesota, Pittsburgh Steelers, Kansas City Chiefs, and Minnesota Vikings. Before becoming a coach, Dungy played three seasons in the NFL.

Dungy has been involved in a wide variety of charitable organizations, including the Fellowship of Christian Athletes, Athletes in Action, Mentors for Life, Big Brothers Big Sisters, Boys & Girls Clubs, the Prison Crusade Ministry, and All Pro Dad. He also works with Basket of Hope, the Black Coaches

Association National Convention, Indiana Black Expo, the United Way of Central Indiana, and the American Diabetes Association.

He and his wife, Lauren, are the parents of six children: daughters, Tiara and Jade, and sons, Eric, Jordan, Justin, and the late James Dungy. They live in Indianapolis, Indiana, and Tampa, Florida.

NATHAN WHITAKER IS the coauthor of *Quiet Strength* and a Harvard Law School graduate whose firm currently represents NFL and college coaches and administrators. A two-sport athlete in baseball and football at Duke University, he has worked in football administration for the Jacksonville Jaguars and Tampa Bay Buccaneers. He has also been employed in ministry. He lives in Florida with his wife, Amy, and their two daughters, Hannah and Ellie Kate.

UN DARE TO BE COMMON™

Visit

www.daretobeuncommon.net

to join others taking the dare, and access

valuable online resources that will inspire

you in uncommon ways.

CP0305

Tony Dungy, NFL head coach and Super Bowl XLI champion, brings together his faith, love of children, and love of sports to tell a story of inspiration and encouragement.

Available everywhere books are sold.